To MARYA
WITH LOVE,

3 - 5 - 99

XX

History Will Absolve Me

Fidel Castro

History Will
Absolve Me

Lyle Stuart Inc.   *Secaucus, N.J.*

1984 edition
Copyright © 1961 by Lyle Stuart
All rights reserved
Published by Citadel Press
A division of Lyle Stuart Inc.
120 Enterprise Ave., Secaucus, N.J. 07094
In Canada: Musson Book Company
A division of General Publishing Co. Limited
Don Mills, Ontario
Manufactured in the United States of America
ISBN 0-8065-0852-3

In memory of the seventy young men who became martyrs of Moncada on July 26, 1953.

* * *

Dedicated to Haydée Santamaria and Melba Hernández, two young women who gave an unforgettable example to all women.

* * *

Presented with a prayer for peace in all the world and with hope that some day soon no one will need to die in order that his people may be free.

Translation of the foreword that appeared in the first edition of "La Historia Me Absolverá," which was clandestinely printed and circulated in June, 1954.

Foreword

We are now approaching the first anniversary of that heroic effort made [July 26, 1953] when a handful of young men armed with little more than their ideals and their self-respect engaged the forces of tyranny in mortal combat. A group of Cuban intellectuals, united in a common cause and inspired by admiration for the 26th of July Movement have decided to publish the complete text of Dr. Fidel Castro's defense plea delivered on October 16th, 1953, before the Emergency Tribunal of Santiago de Cuba.

This publication was made possible through the help of two reporters who attended that memorable session and made available to us the shorthand notes they took there.

Dr. Castro was not tried along with the other accused. The trial in which he undertook his own defense had hardly begun when he was illegally removed from the trial proceedings and prevented from appearing until after the sessions had ended. He was later tried in a room of the City Hospital. With the exception of a few newspapermen, whose reports were completely forbidden by the censorship enforced by National Law, the public was barred from the trial. It was clear that the regime was extraordinarily interested in muffling Dr. Castro's pronouncements. But, despite these circumstances, the speech delivered by Fidel Castro in his own defense is considered the most formidable and courageous indictment yet delivered before a Cuban court of law. It is the most devastating judgment anyone has ever levelled at the present regime of force. The way in which the 26th of July attack was carried out; the revolutionary movement's program; the repulsive crimes perpetrated [by

7

the regime] on the prisoners after the uprising; the shameful and immoral liaison of the Judiciary Department with the Dictatorship; and the principles of law and justice which supported the revolutionaries in their struggle—all this is set forth in a clear and eloquent language which makes no concessions to babbitry or hypocrisies of the present era. The speech offers the incomparable spectacle of a solitary figure consecrated in body and soul, to defend the truth. From the very first paragraph the reader is held entranced and [will not want] to put it down before reading the last paragraph. The reader receives the profound impression that our national problems have been judged in new terms—terms of implacable logic and acuteness which prove his assertions with irrefutable publication of this document is the most formidable reply that can be made to the mediocre and servile American writer who was paid from the public coffers and was provided with an abundance of falsehoods to write the recent biography in praise of Batista—the multimillionaire with a suite at the Waldorf Astorja. That writer, a traitor to the land of Lincoln, glorifies the cruel dictator from the land of Marti. But Batista's true biography and his black role in Cuba's destiny is recorded for posterity in his speech made by Fidel Castro, less to a weak and subservient court than to the tribunal of history.

This twenty-seven-year-old Cuban is today virtually buried alive in a wretched cell on the Isle of Pines, forbidden to speak to another human being, shut off from his country and his family . . . and simply because the regime fears the truth he has written with his sacrifice and martyrdom.

This speech of high moral and idealistic value will also be published abroad, where better printing facilities exist, and it will be distributed throughout the democracies of Latin America as an example of the courage and idealism of Cuban youth—youth who yearned to make their country worthy of the respect and affection with which all Latin America remembered the *Apóstol* during his centenary. Such was their vision that, in their oppressed homeland, they did not hesitate to present him the homage of their own lives.

The Dictator [Batista] denies Cubans their dignity as men. Thus, his hatred and anger for those valiant men who openly defy his power. Seventy young Cubans, cruelly assassinated after the fight, raise their arms from their graves to accuse him, and the

8

voices of twenty-nine living martyrs buried in the somber sheds of the Isle of Pines, are beginning to resound to the heavens demanding punishment of the assassins.

This voice of hope for our country in the midst of today's atmosphere of cowardice and corruption, will grow stronger and louder, no matter how few may speak out for truth in this age of shame. So many of us remain silent, filled with fear and disloyalty to the nation, that we believe a great service will be rendered to the country by publishing the unforgettable words of a Cuban worthy of the name.

To those who, in sinister prisons, are paying so dearly for their devotion to Cuba, we send out the love and hope of their people.

1954, La Habana, Cuba

Preface

On our first encounter—it was in the early Spring of 1957, somewhere in what Herbert Matthews described as "the remote fastnesses" of the Sierra Maestra mountains—Fidel Castro took occasion to tell me about a "little book" that he had written, several years before.

The discussion related, in a manner characteristic of Fidel, to *methods* rather than to abstract ideas. He showed obvious pleasure and no little pride in describing the ingenuity with which, while in solitary confinement and under close guard in a prison cell, he had set down his thoughts, invisibly, in lime juice, between the lines of ordinary letters.

"You would be surprised," he said, "how much trouble it was. I could write for only twenty minutes or so each evening at sunset, when the sun slanted across the paper in such a way as to make the letters visible, glistening on the paper."

The object was to preserve for the Cuban people and for posterity one of the great historical documents of modern times—the complete verbatim transcript of Fidel Castro's speech in his own defense at his trial, October 16, 1953, for conspiracy and armed insurrection

11

against "the constitutional powers of the State"—i.e., against the Batista dictatorship.

The insurrection itself is history. It was launched against the sinister ~~Moncada Barracks~~ in Santiago de Cuba, second most important military establishment on the island, at dawn on July 26, 1953, by a tiny force of Cuban patriots—one hundred sixty-five armed men, two women, under the command of Fidel Castro.

The uprising was crushed. Nearly half of the rebels were killed—most of them tortured to death after capture. The *Movimiento Revolucionario 26 de Julio*—the revolutionary "26th of July" movement that was to destroy the Batista tyranny—was born, rising like a phoenix from the ashes of defeat.

Little more than three years later, Fidel Castro was fighting "hard and successfully," in the Sierra Maestra. On the first day of January, 1959, General Fulgencio Batista y Zaldivar, Cuban "strongman" for more than two decades, fled into exile; and Castro's prediction of six years before was fulfilled. History had, indeed, absolved him.

*La Historia Me Absolverá** has been preserved, not merely the shorthand reporters who were present at his trial.

The trial was conducted in an anteroom of Santiago's Civil Hospital. The public was barred. Press censorship was in force, and the people of Cuba knew little of the proceedings until long afterward.

Fidel's peroration—the "little book" to which he later referred—took five hours to deliver. It is a tribute

*The title is taken from the final phrase of his speech: "Condemn me. History will absolve me."

12

to his eloquence that his judges listened without seeking to interrupt him.

The speech was delivered entirely *ad lib* and without the benefit even of notes. But this in itself is not so extraordinary to those who have become familiar with the revolutionary leader's consummate talent for sustained and brilliant discourse, as the moving and prophetical quality of one man's thought.

La Historia Me Absolverá has proven to be, in effect, both a great social document and an amazingly accurate blueprint of the radical revolutionary program which has changed, inalterably and forever, the lives of six and a half million Cubans, and is at this moment rewriting the history of the Americas and perhaps of the world.

To read it is to become acquainted with the mind, supremely logical, humane, coherent, passionately preoccupied with justice and the human condition, of one of the most remarkable figures ever to grace the American scene.

La Historia Me Absolverá is offered in this edition in response to literally thousands of requests, and in the hope that it will bring new understanding, greatly needed in the United States, of the forces that have shaped the Cuban Revolution and that are changing, day by day, in ways impossible to predict, the future of our own country and of the Western Hemisphere.

ROBERT TABER

13

History Will Absolve Me

Dr. Fidel Castro
appearing before the Emergency Session
of the Court of Santiago de Cuba, Oct. 16, 1953

Honorable Magistrates:

Never has a lawyer had to practice his profession under more difficult conditions; never against an accused have more overwhelming irregularities been committed. Here, counsel and accused are one and the same. As attorney for the defense I have been denied even a look at the indictment. As the accused, I have been, for the past seventy-six days, shut away, in solitary confinement— held incommunicado in violation of every legal and human consideration.

He who is speaking abhors—with all his being— anything that might be vain or childish. Neither by his temperament nor by his present frame of mind is he inclined towards oratorical poses—or towards any kind of sensationalism. I am compelled to plead my own defense before this court. There are two reasons: first, because I have been de prived almost entirely of legal aid; second, because only he who has been outraged as deeply as I, and who has seen his country so forsaken, its justice so reviled, can speak on an occasion like this with words that are made of the blood of his own heart and the very marrow of truth.

There was no lack of generous colleagues who would have defended me and the Bar Association of Havana appointed a courageous and competent jurist, Dr. Jorge Pagliery, Dean of the Bar of this city, to represent me in this case. But he was not permitted to *perform* his

17

undertaking. The prison gates were closed to him as often as he tried to see me. Only after a month and a half, and through the intervention of the Court, was he [finally] granted a ten-minute interview with me in the presence of a sergeant of the Military Intelligence Service. [SIM].[1]

It is taken for granted that a lawyer should converse privately with his client. This right is respected all over the world—except here, where a Cuban prisoner of war is in the hands of an implacable tyranny that abides by no code, legal or humane. Neither Dr. Pagliery nor I were willing to tolerate such spying upon our strategy of defense for the oral trial. Did they, perhaps, want to know in advance how we would reduce to dust the elaborate falsehoods they had woven around the events of *Cuartel Moncada*[2] and how we were going to expose the terrible truths they would go to such very great lengths to conceal? It was then that I decided to make use of my professional status as lawyer. I resolved to assume my own defense.

This decision, first overheard by the sergeant and then reported [to his superiors] provoked among them a singular panic; it seemed as though some mocking little imp were hinting that all their plans might come to naught. You know well enough, Honorable Magistrates, how much pressure has been brought to bear upon me to strip me of the accused man's right to plead his own defense—a right that has been sanctified by long tradi-

[1]Servicio de Inteligencia Militar. Batista's secret political police.
[2]Military garrison near Santiago de Cuba, capital of Oriente Province. This garrison was the object of an unsuccessful attack on the 26th of July, 1953, by Fidel Castro and 165 other young men. The date eventually became the official name of a movement which, four years later was able to depose Batista's regime.

tion in Cuba. The court could not support the government's machinations, for that would have left the accused man altogether undefended. Said accused, who is now exercising this right to do his own pleading, will under no circumstances mute what he ought to say. I deem it essential to cite, at the outset, what was the reason for the relentless isolation to which I have been subjected; what was the motive for keeping me silent; what prompted the plot to kill me—a plot with which the Court is familiar; what grave facts are being hidden from the people; and what is the secret behind all the strange things that have taken place during this trial. All this I propose to do with the utmost clarity.

2

You have publicly called this case the most significant in the history of the Republic. If you sincerely believed so, you should not have allowed the trial to be degraded, time after time, by the flouting of your authority.

The first court session was held on the 21st of September. Scandalously invading the courtroom were a hundred [soldiers armed with] machine guns and bayonets. They surrounded the more than a hundred persons seated in the prisoner's dock. The majority of these accused had in no way been involved in our acts. They had been under preventive arrest for many days, after suffering all kinds of outrage and abuse in the chambers of the repressive organizations. The rest of the gallant and determined accused were eager and proud to confirm the roles that were theirs in the battle for freedom: to offer an example of unusual self-sacrifice, and to deliver from the jaws of jail the ones whom [the regime] with deliberate bad faith, had included in the trial. Men who had fought each other came face to face once more. Once again, with the cause of justice on our side, we would wage the mighty battle of truth against infamy. Surely, the regime was not prepared for the moral catastrophe in store for it.

How could the regime maintain its false accusations? How could it keep secret all that had really transpired, while so many young men were willing to run *any* risk—jail, torture, death, if need be—to denounce [the Army's acts] before the court?

In the first session, I was a witness. For two hours I was questioned by the court's prosecutor as well as by twenty defense attorneys. I was able to prove with exact facts and figures the sums of money that had been invested, the way in which this money was collected, and the arms that we had managed to assemble. I had nothing to hide since all this was achieved by a self-abnegation unsurpassed in the struggles of our Republic. I spoke of the aims which inspired us in our struggle and of the humane and generous treatment that we had at all times accorded to our adversaries. If I accomplished my purpose of demonstrating the non-involvement, direct or indirect, of those men who were falsely implicated in this trial, I owe it to the complete support and backing of my heroic comrades. For, as I said, mere concern over consequences would not make them regret or repent being rebels and patriots. I was never allowed to talk with them in prison; yet we were in full accord as to how to proceed. When men bear the same ideals in their hearts, nothing can keep them incommunicado: neither walls of prisons nor sod of cemeteries. For a single memory, a single spirit, a single idea, a single conscience, a single dignity, will sustain them all.

From that moment on, the structure of lies the regime had erected around Camp Moncada began to collapse like a house of cards. As a result, the prosecutor understood how absurd it was to keep in prison all those persons named as instigators. Immediately he demanded their provisional release.

At the close of my testimony in that first session, I asked that the court allow me to leave the dock and sit among the counsel for the defense; this permission was, in effect, granted to me. At this point began what I considered my most important mission in this trial: utterly to discredit the cowardly, base and treacherous—shameless!—slanders that the regime had hurled against our fighters; to reveal with irrefutable evidence the frightful, repulsive crimes they had practiced on those of our companions whom they captured; and to bring before the nation and the world the infinite misfortune of Cuba's people, who are now enduring the most cruel—the most inhuman—oppression in all their history.

The second session convened on Tuesday, September the twenty-second. After only ten witnesses had testified, I was able to call attention to the murders in the Manzanillo[1] region. I specifically established and placed on record the direct responsibility of the captain commanding that post. There were three hundred more

[1] Large port town in the south-western sector of Oriente Province where some of the fiercest battles between Castro's men and Batista's soldiers took place.

witnesses to testify. What would happen when—with a staggering mass of facts and evidence—I should proceed to cross-examine the very Army men who were directly responsible for those crimes? Could the regime permit me to go ahead—before the large audience in attendance? Before journalists and jurists from all the island? And before the opposition party leaders, whom it had stupidly seated right in the prisoner's dock where they could now hear so distinctly all that might be brought out here? The regime would have dynamited the courthouse—with all its magistrates—rather than allow this!

They devised a plan to eliminate me from the trial and proceeded to do so *manu militari*. Friday night, the 25th of September, on the eve of the third session of the trial, two prison doctors visited me in my cell. They were visibly embarrassed. "We have come to examine you," they told me. I asked: "Who is so concerned about my health?" Actually, from the moment I first saw them, I realized what they had in mind. They could not have treated me with greater chivalry, and they explained [their predicament] to me. In the afternoon, Colonel Chaviano[2] had appeared at the prison and had told them I "was doing the Government terrible damage at the trial." He had said they must sign a certificate declaring that I was ill—and, was, therefore, unable to come to court. The doctors told me that they—for their part, were prepared to resign from their posts and to risk persecution. They put the matter in my hands, for me to decide. I found it hard to ask those men to destroy them-

[2]Colonel Alberto del Rio Chaviano. Commander of the Army in the Manzanillo sector.

selves without vacillation. But neither could I, under any circumstances, consent that their orders be carried out. To leave the matter to their own consciences, I answered only: "You must know your duty; I surely know mine."

After leaving my cell they signed the certificate. I know they did so, believing in good faith, that this was the only way they could save my life—which they considered to be in the greatest danger. I was not obliged to keep our conversation secret, for I am bound only by truth. Telling the truth in this instance may jeopardize those good physicians in their material interests. But I am removing all doubt about their honor—and that is worth much more. The same night, I wrote the court a letter denouncing the plot; requesting two forensic physicians be sent to certify my excellent state of health, and informing you that if, to save my life, I should need to collaborate in such a deception, I would a thousand times prefer to lose it. To show my resolve to fight alone against all this low conniving, I added to my own words a concept of the *Maestro*.[3] A rightful cause, from the depths of a cave, can accomplish more than [any] army."

As the court is aware, Dr. Melba Hernandez[4] submitted that letter at the third session of the trial, September twenty-sixth. I managed to get it to her despite the unrelenting watch under which I was kept. That letter, of course, caused immediate reprisals: Dr. Hernandez was subjected to solitary confinement, and I—since I was already incommunicado—was sent to the

[3]Refers to Jose Martí (1853–1895) Cuban author and patriot in the War of Independence emancipating Cuba from Spanish rule.
[4]One of the two girls who took part in the 26th of July attack on Cuartel Moncada.

most inaccessible part of the prison. From that time on, all the accused were painstakingly searched, head to foot, before they were brought to the courtroom.

Two court physicians [examined me] September twenty-seventh and certified I was, in fact, in perfect health. And yet, in spite of the court's repeated orders, never again was I brought to the trial sessions. Moreover, every day, anonymous persons circulated hundreds of apocryphal pamphlets in which there was [preposterous] talk of my rescue from jail. This stupid alibi was invented to explain—as escape!—the abduction they intended. Since the scheme failed as a result of timely exposure by my alert friends, and after the first medical affidavit was revealed to be false, [the regime] could keep me away from the trial only by open and shameless contempt of court.

An unheard-of situation had arisen, Honorable Magistrates. Here was a regime afraid to bring an accused before the courts; a regime of blood and terror which shrank in fear at the moral conviction of a defenseless man—unarmed, slandered and isolated. Thus, having deprived me of all else, they finally deprived me of the trial in which I was the principal accused.

Bear in mind that this was during a period of suspension of rights of the individual and while there was in full force the Law of Public Order as well as censorship of radio and press. What dreadful crimes this regime must have committed, to so fear the voice of one accused man!

3

I must dwell upon the insolence and disrespect which the army leaders have, at all times, shown toward you. As often as this court has outlawed the inhuman isolation in which I was held; as often as it has ordered my most elementary rights to be respected; as often as it has demanded that I be brought before it, this court was never obeyed! One after another, all its orders were disregarded. Worse yet: in the very presence of the court, during the first and second sessions, a praetorian guard was stationed beside me to prevent me completely from speaking to anyone, even during the brief recesses. In other words, not only in prison, but even in the very courtroom and in your presence, they ignored your decrees. I had intended to mention this matter in the following session, as a question of elementary respect for the court, but . . . I was never brought back. And when, in exchange for so much disrespect, they bring us before you, to be sent to jail in the name of a statute which they—and only they—have been violating since the 10th of March, sad indeed is the role they would force upon you. The Latin maxim, *cedant arma togae*,[1] has certainly not been fulfilled on a single occasion during this case. I beg you to keep that circumstance well in mind.

Furthermore, these devices were, after all, quite useless; my brave comrades, with unprecedented patriotism, did their duty to the utmost.

"Yes, we set out to fight for Cuba's freedom and we do not regret having done it," they declared, one by one, on the witness stand. Then, addressing the court with

[1]Let arms yield to the toga.

25

imposing courage, they denounced the hideous crimes practiced upon the bodies of our brothers. Although absent from court, I was able, in my prison cell, to follow the trial in all its details; (for this I must thank the convicts at Boniato Prison). Despite all threats, these men found ingenious means to get newspaper clippings and all kinds of information into my hands. In this way, they avenged the abuses and immoralities of both the warden Taboada and the supervisor, Lieutenant Rozabal, who [not only] drive them from dawn to dusk building private mansions, but moreover starve them by embezzling the prison food budget.

As the trial progressed, roles were reversed: those who came to accuse found themselves accused, and the accused became the accusers! It was not the revolutionaries who were judged there; judged once and for all time was a man named Batista[2] . . . MONSTRUM HORRENDUM! . . . It matters less that those worthy and valiant young men have been condemned, if tomorrow the people will condemn the Dictator and his henchmen. Our men were consigned to the Isle of Pines Prison, in whose circular galleries the ghost of Castell[3] lingers on, and where the cries of countless victims echo yet; there our boys have been sent to expiate their love of liberty—in bitter confinement, sequestered away from society, torn from their homes and banished from their country. [Now that they are disposed of] do you not believe—as I said before—that it is difficult and thankless for their lawyer to finish [their defense]?

As a result of so many obscure and illegal machina-

[2]Fulgencio Batista Zaldivar.
[3]Notorious Isle of Pines warden who murdered prisoners there.

tions, due to the *will* of those who govern and the *weakness* of those who judge, I find myself here in this little room[4] of the Civil Hospital—to which I have been brought to be tried in secret; so that my voice may be stifled and so that no one may learn of the things I am going to say. Why, then, do we need that imposing Palace of Justice which the Honorable Magistrates would without doubt find rather more comfortable? I must warn you: it is unwise to administer justice from a hospital room, surrounded by sentinels with bayonets fixed; the citizens might suppose that our justice is sick . . . and that it is captive . . .

I remind you, your laws of procedure provide that trials shall be "both audible and public;" however, the people have been barred altogether from this session of court. The only civilians admitted here have been two attorneys and six reporters, whose newspapers censorship will prevent from printing a word that I say. I see, as my sole audience, in this chamber and in the corridors, nearly a hundred soldiers and officers. I am grateful for the polite and serious attention they give me. I only wish I could have the whole Army before me! I know, one day this army will seethe with rage to wash away the awful, the shameful bloodstains splattered across the uniform by the present ruthless clique in their lust for power. On that day, oh, what a fall awaits those mounted, in arrogance, on the backs of the noble soldiers!—provided, that is, that the people have not pulled them down long before!

Finally, I should like to add that no treatise on penal law was allowed to be brought to my cell. I have at my

[4]Nurses' lounge in the hospital.

27

disposal just this tiny code of law lent to me by my learned counsel, Dr. Baudilio Castellanos, the courageous defender of my comrades. In the same way they prohibited me from receiving the books of Marti; it seems the prison censorship considered them too subversive. Or is it because I named Martí as the instigator of the 26th of July?

I was also prevented from bringing to this trial reference books on any other subject. It makes no difference whatsoever! I carry in my heart the teachings of the *Maestro* and in my mind the noble ideas of all men who have [ever] defended the freedom of the peoples of the world!

I am going to make only one request of this court; I trust it will be granted as a compensation for the many abuses and outrages the accused has had to tolerate without protection of the law. I ask that my right to express myself be respected without restraint. Otherwise, even the merest semblance of justice cannot be maintained, and the last episode [of this trial] would be, more than any other, one of ignominy and cowardice.

4

I must confess that I am somewhat disappointed. I had expected that the Honorable Prosecutor would come forward with a grave accusation. I thought he would be ready to justify, to the limit, his contention— and his reasons why—I should be condemned in the name of Law and Justice (what law and what justice?) to twenty-six years in prison. But no. He has confined himself to an oral reading of Article 148 of the Social Defense Code. On the basis of this, plus aggravating circumstances, he demands I be imprisoned for the considerable term of twenty-six years! Two minutes seems very little time in which to demand and justify that a man be put behind bars for more than a quarter of a century. Can it be that the Honorable Prosecutor is, perhaps, annoyed with the court? Because, as I see it, his laconic attitude in this case mocks the solemnity with which the Honorable Magistrates declared, rather proudly, that this was a trial of great importance! I have seen prosecutors speak ten times longer in a simple narcotics case asking a sentence of only six months. The Honorable Prosecutor has supplied not a word in support of his petition. I am a just man . . . I realize that for a prosecuting attorney under oath of fidelity to the Constitution of the Republic, it is difficult to come here in the name of an unconstitutional, *de facto* government, lacking any legal—much less moral—basis, and ask that a young Cuban, a lawyer like himself, perhaps as honorable as he, be sent to jail for twenty-six years. But the Honorable Prosecutor is a gifted man and I have seen much less talented persons write lengthy diatribes in defense of this regime. How, then, can I suppose that he lacks reasons with which to defend it, at least for fifteen minutes, however, contemptible that might be to any decent person? There can be no doubt that there is some noteworthy conspiracy behind all this.

5

HONORABLE MAGISTRATES: Why such inter-
est in keeping me quiet? Why forego those arguments
that could serve as a target against which I might direct
my own brief? Is it that they lack any legal, moral, and
political foundations on which to base a serious statement of the question? Are they so afraid of the truth? Do
they hope that I, too, will speak for only two minutes and
that I will not here touch upon the points which have
caused certain persons sleepless nights since the 26th of
July? Since the prosecutor's petition was restricted to
the mere reading of five lines of an article of the Social
Defense Code,[1] they might suppose that I would limit
myself to these same lines and circle round and round
them, like a slave turning a millstone. But I shall by no
means accept such a gag, for in this trial there is at stake
much more than the freedom of a single individual. Fundamental matters of principle are being debated here,
the right of men to be free is on trial, the very foundations of our existence as a civilized and democratic nation
are in the balance. When this trial is over, I do not want
to have to reproach myself for any principle left
undefended, for any truth left unsaid, for any crime left
unnamed.

The Honorable Prosecutor's famous little article deserves hardly a minute of my time. I shall limit myself,
for the moment, to a brief juridical skirmish against it,
because I want to clear the field for an attack against all
of the endless lies and deceits, the hypocrisy, the bab-
bittry, and the moral cowardice that set the stage for the

[1]Created at the time of the Constitution of 1940.

crude comedy which, since the 10th of March—and even before then—has been called Justice in Cuba.

It is a fundamental principle of Penal Law that an imputed offense must correspond exactly to the offense as described in the law. If no law applies exactly to the controversial point, there is no offense.

The article in question says textually: "A penalty of imprisonment of from three to ten years shall be imposed upon the perpetrator of any act aimed at bringing about an armed uprising against the CONSTITUTIONAL POWERS OF THE STATE. The penalty shall be imprisonment for from five to twenty years, in case the insurrection actually be carried into effect.

[handwritten margin notes: lawyer / must know laws in order to truly see the Truth and injustice]

In what country is the Honorable Prosecutor living? Who has told him that we have sought to bring about an uprising against the CONSTITUTIONAL POWERS OF THE STATE? Two things are self-evident. In the first place, the dictatorship that oppresses the nation is not a CONSTITUTIONAL POWER, but an unconstitutional one; it was established against the Constitution, over the head of the Constitution, violating the legitimate Constitution of the Republic. The legitimate Constitution is that which emanates directly from a sovereign people. I shall demonstrate this point more fully later on, notwithstanding all the subterfuges contrived by cowards and traitors to justify the unjustifiable. In the second place, the article speaks of Powers, in the plural, not the singular, because it refers to the case of a republic governed [jointly] by a Legislative Power, an Executive Power and a Judicial Power which balance and counterbalance one another. We have fomented a rebellion against one single power, an illegal power, which has usurped and merged into a single whole both the Legis-

31

lative and Executive Powers of the nation, and has thus destroyed the entire system that was specifically safeguarded by the Code now under our analysis. As to the independence of the Judiciary after the 10th of March, I shall not allude to that for I am in no mood for joking. No matter how Article 148 may be stretched, shrunk or amended, not a single comma applies to the events of the 26th of July. Let us leave this statute alone [just now] and await the opportunity to apply it to those who really *did* foment uprising against the Constitutional Powers of the State. Later, I shall refer back to the Code to refresh the Honorable Prosecutor's memory about certain circumstances he has unfortunately overlooked.

I warn you: I have just begun! If there is in your hearts a vestige of love for your country, of love for humanity, of love for justice, listen attentively to me. I know I will be silenced for many years; I know [the regime] will try to suppress the truth by all possible means; I know there will be a conspiracy to sink me into oblivion. But my voice will not be stifled; strength gathers in my breast even when I feel most alone, and the ardour of my own heart can sustain my voice, no matter how callous cowards may isolate and try to discourage me.

6

I listened to [the radio broadcast[1] by] the dictator on Monday, July 27th, from a shack in the mountains, while there were still eighteen of our men in arms against the Government. Those who never experience similar moments will never be acquainted with bitterness and indignation in life. While the long-cherished hopes of freeing our people lay in ruins about us, we heard those crushed hopes gloated over by a tyrant more vicious, more arrogant, than ever. The endless stream of lies and slanders poured out in his crude, odious, repulsive language must be compared with the endless stream of clean young blood which had flowed since the previous night—flowed with his knowledge, consent, complicity and applause—being spilled by the most inhuman gang of assassins it is possible to imagine. To have believed him for one single minute should suffice to fill a man of conscience with remorse, for the rest of his life. At that moment I could not even hope to brand his miserable forehead with [the] mark of truth which condemns him for the rest of his days and for all time to come; already there was closing in around us a net of more than a thousand men, armed with weapons more powerful than ours and with peremptory orders to bring in our bodies. Now that people are beginning to learn the truth, now that—speaking before you—I am completing the mission I then set myself, I will be able to die peaceful and content. So I shall not mince words about the savage murderers.

Let us pause to consider the facts. The government said the attack showed such precision and perfection that

[1]From Camp Columbia, Havana.

military strategists must have done the planning. Nothing could be further from the truth. The plan was pre pared by a group of young men, none of whom had any military experience; I am going to reveal their names, omitting those of two boys still alive and free: Abel Santamaria, Jose Luis Tasende, Renato Guitar Rosell, Pedro Miret, Jesus Montané and this speaker. Half are dead, and in the tribute due their memory I can say that although they were *not* military experts, they had patriotism enough that—had we not been under such great disadvantages—they could have given a good beating to the entire lot of generals of the 10th of March—those generals who are neither soldiers nor patriots.

Much more difficult than planning the attack was our organization, training, mobilizing and arming of men during this repressive regime with its millions of dollars spent on espionage, bribery and informers. Nevertheless, all our undertaking was accomplished—by the young men just mentioned and by many others like them—with incredible earnestness, discretion and constancy. Still, most praiseworthy, always, is their giving to an ideal, everything they had—ultimately, giving their very lives.

The final mobilization of men who came to this province from the most remote towns of the entire island was accomplished with admirable precision and in absolute secrecy. It is equally true that the attack was carried out with magnificent coordination. It began simultaneously at 5:15 A.M., in both Bayamo[2] and Santiago de

[2]Large and historically significant town in the fertile region of the Cauto valley. The Cuban National Anthem was originally written in honor of the gallant *Bayameses* who joined the rebellious forces with a battle cry known as "el Grito de Baire" of 1895.

Cuba; and one by one, with an exactitude of minutes and seconds foreseen in advance, the buildings surrounding the barracks fell to our forces. Nevertheless, in the interests of accuracy, and even though it may detract from our reputation, I am also going to reveal a fact that was fatal: due to a most unfortunate error, half of our forces— and the better armed half, at that—went astray at the entrance to the city and were not on hand to help us at the decisive moment. Abel Santamaria, with twenty-one men, had occupied the City Hospital; with him went a doctor and two of our girl comrades, to attend the wounded. Raul Castro, with ten men, occupied the Palace of Justice and it was my responsibility to attack the barracks with the rest, ninety-five men. Preceded by an advance guard of eight who had forced Gate Three, I arrived with the first group of forty-five men. It was precisely here that the battle began, when my automobile ran into a perimeter patrol armed with machine-guns. The reserve group, who had almost all the heavy weapons [the light arms were in the advance guard] turned up the wrong street and lost their way in this city, with which they were not familiar. I must clarify that I do not for a moment doubt the valour of those men; they experienced great anguish and desperation when they realized they were lost. Because of the type of action under way and because of the identical color of the uniforms of the two contending forces, it was not easy for these men to reestablish contact with us. Many of them, captured later on, met death with true heroism.

We all had strict instructions to be, above all, humane in the struggle. Never was a group of armed men more generous to the adversary. From the very first, we took numerous prisoners—eventually nearly twenty—

and there was one moment when three of our men—
Ramiro Valdes, Jose Suarez and Jesus Montane—
managed to enter a barracks and hold nearly fifty soldiers
prisoners for a short time. Those soldiers have testified
before the court, and all without exception have acknowledged that we treated them with absolute respect,
without even offending them by the use of an unpleasant
word. Apropos of this, I want to give the prosecutor my
heartfelt thanks for one thing in the trial of my comrades:
When he made his report, he was fair enough to ac-
knowledge as an incontestable fact that we maintained a
high spirit of chivalry throughout the struggle.

Discipline among the soldiers was very poor. They
finally defeated us, because of their superiority in numbers—fifteen to one—and because of the protection af-
forded them by the defenses of the fortress. Our men
were much the better marksmen, as our enemies con-
ceded. Courage was high on both sides.

In reflecting on the causes for our tactical failure,
apart from the regrettable error already mentioned, I
believe we made a mistake by dividing the commando
unit we had so carefully trained. Of our best trained men
and boldest leaders, there were 27 in Bayamo, 21 in the
City Hospital and 10 in the Palace of Justice. If our forces
had been otherwise distributed, the outcome of the battle might have been different. The clash with the patrol
(purely accidental, since the unit would not have been at
that point twenty seconds earlier or twenty seconds
later) alerted the camp and gave them time to mobilize.
Otherwise the camp would have fallen without a shot
since the guard post was already in our control. On the
other hand, except for the .22 calibre rifles, for which

there were plenty of bullets, our side was very short of ammunition. Had we had hand grenades, the Army would not have been able to resist us for fifteen minutes.

When I became convinced that all efforts to take the fort had now become quite futile, I began to withdraw our men in groups of eight and ten. Our retreat was covered by six expert marksmen under the command of Pedro Miret and Fidel Labrador; heroically they impeded the Army's advance. Our losses in the battle had been insignificant; 95% of our casualties came from the army's inhumanity *after* the struggle. The group in the City Hospital had but one casualty; the rest of that group were trapped when the troops blocked that building's one exit; but our boys did not lay down their arms until their very last bullet was gone. With them was Abel Santamaria, the most generous, beloved, and intrepid of our young men, whose glorious resistance immortalizes him in the history of Cuba. We shall see the fate they met and how Batista sought to castigate the heroism of our youth.

Our plans were to continue the struggle in the mountains in case the attack on the regiment were to fail. In Siboney I was able to gather together a third of our forces; but many of these men were now discouraged. About twenty of them decided to surrender; later we shall see what became of them. The rest, eighteen men, with what arms and ammunition was left, followed me into the mountains. The terrain was completely unknown to us. For one week we held the heights of the Gran Piedra range and the Army occupied the foothills. We could not come down, and they could not decide to come up. It was not force of arms but hunger and thirst that ultimately overcame our resistance. I had to divide the men into smaller groups. Some managed to slip through the Army lines; others were escorted in to be surrendered by Monsignor Perez Serantes.[3] Finally, only two companions remained with me: Jose Suarez and Oscar Alcalde. While the three of us were totally exhausted, a force led by Lieutenant Sarria surprised us in our sleep at dawn. This was Saturday, August the first. The slaughter of prisoners had ceased now, as a result of tremendous protest by the people. This officer, a man of honor, saved us from being murdered on the spot, with our hands tied [behind us].

I need not deny here the statements by Ugalde Carrillo and company, who tried to blacken my name in an effort to mask their own cowardice, incompetence, and criminality. The facts are clear enough.

My purpose is not to detain the court with epic narrations. All I have said is essential for the more exact understanding of the rest of my plea.

Let me mention two facts that enable objective judgment of our attitude. First: to facilitate capture of the regiment we could simply have seized all the high ranking officers in their homes. This possibility was rejected for the very humane reason that we wished to avoid scenes of tragedy and struggle in the presence of their families. Second: we agreed not to take over any radio station until the Army camp was in our power. This attitude, uncommonly gallant and magnanimous, spared the citizens much bloodshed. With only ten men I could

has the
Right.

[3]Archbishop of Santiago. He sympathized with and actively supported the struggle against Batista; his intervention obtained promise of trial for Castro and a few other young men who had escaped the torture and murder of rebels immediately following their July 26th attempt.

have seized a radio station, to draw the people into the revolt. The people's will to fight could not be questioned. I had a recording of Eduardo Chibás[4] last message on C.M.Q. [I also had] patriotic poems and battle hymns capable of moving the least sensitive—especially with the sound of battle in their ears. But I did not want to use [these incitements] although our situation was desperate.

7

The regime has emphatically repeated that our movement did not have popular support. I have never heard an assertion so naive, and at the same so full of bad faith. The regime seeks to show the submission and cowardice of the people. They almost claim that the people support the Dictatorship; they do not know how this pretense offends the brave *Orientales*. Santiago thought our attack was only a local disturbance between two factions of soldiers; not until many hours later, did they realize what had happened. Who can doubt the valour, the civic pride and the limitless courage of the rebel and patriotic people of Santiago de Cuba? If Moncada had fallen into our hands, even the women of Santiago de Cuba would have shouldered arms. Many were the rifles loaded for

[4]Cuban senator, leader of the *Partido del Pueblo Cubano* (Cuban Peoples' Party), also known as the *Ortodoxo* Party. He was a favorite candidate in the presidential campaign of 1952. Chibás, in a wave of depression provoked by the political apathy of the people and by sedition in his own ranks, took his own life shortly before the coup of the 10th of March.

our fighters by the nurses of the City Hospital! They fought alongside us. That is something we shall never forget.

It was never our intention to engage the soldiers of the regiment in combat, but to seize control and weapons by surprise, to arouse the people and then call the soldiers together. We would have invited them to abandon the flag of tyranny and to embrace the banner of Liberty; to defend the supreme interests of the nation and not the petty interests of a small group; to turn their guns around and fire on the enemies of the people and not fire on the people, among whom are their own sons and fathers; to join with the people themselves, brothers of ours that they are, instead of opposing the people as the enemies the government tried to make of them; to march behind the only beautiful ideal worthy of the sacrifice of one's life—the greatness and the happiness of one's country. To those who doubt that many soldiers would have followed us, I ask: What Cuban does not cherish glory? What heart is not set aflame by the dawn of freedom?

The Navy did not fight against us, and it would undoubtedly have come over to our side later. It is known that that branch of the Armed Forces is the least dominated by the Dictatorship and that there is a very intense civic conscience among its members. But, as regards the rest of the national armed forces, would they have fought against a people in revolt? I declare that they would not! A soldier is made of flesh and blood; he thinks, observes and feels. He is susceptible to the opinions, beliefs, sympathies and antipathies of the people. If you ask his opinion he may tell you he cannot express it; but that does not mean he has no opinion. He is affected by exactly the same problems that affect other citizens: subsistence, rent, the education of his children, their future, etc. Every one of his kin is an inevitable point of contact between him and the people and everyone of his kin relates him to the present and future situation of the society in which he lives. It is foolish to presume that the salary a soldier receives from the State—a modest enough salary, moreover—should solve the vital problems posed for him by his needs, duties and sentiments as a member of his family and as a member of his community.

This brief explanation has been necessary because it is fundamental to a consideration to which few people, until now, have paid any attention: soldiers have a profound respect for the sentiments of the majority of the people! During the Machado[5] regime, in the same proportion as popular antipathy increased, the loyalty of the Army visibly decreased. This was so true that a group of women almost succeeded in subverting Camp Columbia. But this is proved even more clearly by a recent development. While Grau San Martin's regime[6] was able to preserve its maximum popularity among the people, unscrupulous ex-officers and power-hungry civilians attempted innumerable conspiracies in the Army. But none of them found a following in the rank and file.

[5]Gerardo Machado y Morales. Originally elected during the sugar boom (1924). Gerardo Machado was a popular president who turned out to be a Dr. Jekyll and Mr. Hyde, assuming dictatorial powers in 1928 and precipitating a period of bloody civil strife which ended in 1933.

[6]Ramon Grau San Martin, acknowledged leader of the liberal movement that grew around the nucleus of intellectuals who fought against Machado. Grau's party, after an unsuccessful try in 1934, was constitutionally elected in 1944.

8

The coup of the 10th of March[1] occurred at the moment when the civil government's prestige had dwindled to its lowest ebb, a circumstance of which Batista and his clique took advantage. Why did they not strike their blow after the first of June? Simply because, had they waited for the majority of the nation to express its will at the polls, the troops would not have responded to the conspiracy!

Consequently, a second assertion can be made: the Army has never revolted against a regime with a popular majority behind it. These are historic truths, and if Batista insists on remaining in power at all costs against the will of the majority of Cubans, his end will be more tragic than that of Gerardo Machado.

I have the right to express an opinion about the Armed Forces; I defended them when everyone else was silent. And I did this neither as a conspirator, nor from any kind of personal interest (for we then enjoyed full constitutional prerogatives). I was prompted only by humane instincts and civic duty. In those days, the newspaper "Alerta" was one of the most widely read because of its position in national politics. In its pages, I campaigned against the forced labor to which the soldiers were subjected on the private estates of high civil and military figures. On the third of March, 1952, I supplied the courts with data, photographs, films and other proofs denouncing this state of affairs. I also pointed out in those articles that it was elementary decency to increase

[1] 10th of March, 1952, date of military coup by which Batista seized control of the government; near the close of Prios' term as elected president.

42

Army pay. I should like to know who else raised his voice on that occasion to protest against [all the] injustice done the soldiers. Certainly not Batista and Company,[2] living well-protected on their luxurious estates, surrounded by all kinds of security measures, while I ran a thousand risks without either bodyguards or arms.

Just as I defended the soldiers then, now—when all others are again silent—I tell the soldiers that they allowed themselves to be miserably deceived; and to the deception and shame of the 10th of March, they have added the disgrace—a thousand times greater disgrace—of the frightful and unjustifiable crimes of Santiago de Cuba. Since that time, the uniform of the Army remains degraded. Just as last year I told the people, and decried before the courts, that soldiers were working as slaves on private estates, so today I make the bitter charge that there are soldiers stained through and through with the blood of the Cuban youths they have tortured and slain. And I also say that when the Army serves the Republic, defends the nation, respects the people, and protects every citizen, it is only fair that the soldier should earn at least a hundred dollars a month. But when the soldiers slay and oppress the people, betray the nation and defend the interests of one clique; the Army deserves not a cent of the Republic's money and that Camp Columbia should be converted into a school with ten thousand orphans installed there, instead of soldiers.

[2]At this time Batista was senator in Cuba and also a candidate for the presidency in forthcoming elections.

43

9

Since, above all things, I wish to be just, I cannot blame all the soldiers for the crimes and the shame that is the work of a few Army men who are evil and treacherous. However, every honorable and upstanding soldier who loves his career and his uniform is dutybound to demand and to fight for the cleansing of this guilt, for the avenging of his betrayal, and for the punishment of the guilty. Otherwise, the soldier's uniform will be forever a mark of infamy, instead of a source of pride.

Naturally, the 10th of March regime had no choice but to remove the soldiers from private estates. But Batista did so only to put them to work as porters, chauffeurs, servants and bodyguards to the whole rabble of petty politicians who form the party of the Dictatorship. Every fourth or fifth rank official considers himself entitled to the services of a soldier—to drive his car and to shield his back, as though he were constantly afraid of receiving the kick he so richly deserves.

If there had been any real intention of reform, why did the regime not confiscate all the estates and the millions [of pesos] from men like Genovevo Perez Damera,[1] who acquired their fortunes exploiting soldiers, driving them like slaves, and misappropriating the funds of the Armed Forces? But no; Genovevo and the others no doubt still have soldiers protecting them on their estates because, the generals of the 10th of March,

---

[1]Genovevo Perez, Chief of Staff under both Grau San Martin and Prio Socarras, was largely responsible for the Cuban Army's demoralization, which facilitated Batista's *coup* in 1952.

deep down inside, expect to follow their example. The regime dared not set a precedent of punishment.

The 10th of March was indeed a miserable deception. After Batista and his band of corrupt and disreputable politicians had failed in their electoral plans, they took advantage of the Army's discontent and used it to climb to power on the backs of the soldiers. I know there are many [Army] men disgruntled because they have been disappointed. At first, their pay was raised; but later, by means of deductions and reductions of every kind, it was lowered again; many of the old elements, which had drifted away from the Armed Forces, returned to the ranks and blocked the advancement of young, capable and valuable men. Good soldiers have been neglected while the most scandalous nepotism prevails. Many decent military men are now asking themselves what need had the Armed Forces to assume the tremendous historical responsibility of destroying our Constitution, merely to put in power a group of immoral men. [Especially these] men of bad reputation, corrupt, politically degenerate beyond redemption, who could never again have occupied a political post had it not been at the point of bayonets—furthermore, bayonets they did not even wield themselves!

The soldiers endure a tyranny even worse than the civilians. They are under constant surveillance and not one of them enjoys the slightest security in his post. Any unjustified suspicion, any gossip, any intrigue, or denunciation, is sufficient to cause transfer, dismissal or dishonorable imprisonment. Did not Tabernilla,[2] in a circular, forbid them to talk with any one opposed to the

[2]General Francisco Tabernilla. Chief of Police under Batista.

government—that is to say, with ninety-nine percent of the people? What distrust! Not even the Vestal Virgins of Rome were required to observe such a rule! As for the widely publicized soldier's housing, there are no more than 500 in all the island; and yet, with what has been spent on tanks, guns and other weapons there would have been enough money to build a house for each enlisted man.

What concerns Batista is not to take care of the Army, but that the Army should take care of him! To augment the Army's power of oppression and killing is not to increase well-being among the soldiers. Triple guard duty, constant confinement to barracks, continual anxiety, the enmity of the people, uncertainty about the future—that's what has been given the soldier. In other words: "Die for the regime, soldier, give it your sweat and blood. We shall dedicate a speech to you and award you a posthumous promotion (when it no longer matters) and afterwards—we shall go on living luxuriously, making ourselves rich. Kill, abuse, oppress the people. When the people grow weary and all this comes to an end, you shall pay for our crimes, while we go abroad to live like princes. And if, one day, we return, do not knock—neither you nor your children—on the doors of our mansions, for we shall be millionaires, and millionaires do not know the poor. Kill, soldier, oppress the people, die for the regime, give your sweat and blood . . ."

10

But, if blind to that sad reality, a minority of soldiers had decided to fight the people—the people who were going to liberate them too from tyranny—still victory would have gone to the people. The Honorable Prosecutor was very much interested in knowing our chances for success. These chances were based on considerations of technical, military and social orders. There has been an attempt to establish the myth that modern arms render the people helpless to overthrow tyrants. Military parades and the pompous display of the machines of war are utilized to perpetuate this myth and to create in the people a complex of absolute impotence. But no weapon, no violence can vanquish the people once they have decided to win back their rights. Both past and present are full of examples. Most recently there has been the revolt in Bolivia, where miners with dynamite sticks laid low the Regular Army regiments. But, fortunately, we Cubans need not look for examples abroad. No example is as inspiring as that of our own land. During the war of 1895 there were nearly half a million armed Spanish soldiers in Cuba—many more than the Dictator counts upon today to hold back a population five times greater. The arms of the Spanish were, beyond comparison, both more up-to-date and more powerful than those of the patriots. In many of the contests, [the Spanish] were equipped with field artillery and the infantry used carbines similar to those still in use by the infantry of today. The Cubans were armed only with their machetes, for their cartridge belts were nearly always empty. There is an unforgettable passage in the story of our war of independence, narrated by General

47

Miro Argentes,[1] Chief of State for Antonio Maceo.[2] I managed to bring it copied on this little note, in order not to depend upon memory.

"Untrained men under the command of Pedro Delgado, most of them equipped only with machetes, were virtually annihilated as they threw themselves on the solid ranks of Spaniards. It is not an exaggeration to assert that of every fifty men, twenty-five were killed. Some even attacked the Spaniards with bare fists, without pistols, without machetes, without even knives. Searching through the reeds by the Hondo River, fifteen more dead of the Cuban party were found and it was not immediately evident to what group they belonged. They did not appear to have shouldered arms, their clothes were intact and only tin drinking cups hung from their waists; a few steps ahead lay a dead Spanish horse, all its equipment intact. We reconstructed the climax of the tragedy. These men, following their daring chief, Lieutenant Colonel Pedro Delgado, had earned heroes' laurels; they had thrown themselves against bayonets with bare hands; the clash of metal which was heard around them was the sound of their drinking cups banging against the saddle-horn."

Maceo was deeply moved. This man so accustomed to seeing death in all its forms, murmured this praise: "I had never seen this—untrained and unarmed men, attacking the Spaniards with only a drinking cup for a weapon. And I called it an *impedimenta!*"

[1]Catalonian general who became one of the leaders of the War of Independence. Father of Dr. Miró Cardona, the first premier of the present Revolutionary government.

[2]1848–1896 The "Titan of Bronze", the most spectacular warrior of Cuba's War of Independence.

This is how the people fight when they want to win their liberty; they throw stones at airplanes and overturn tanks!

11

As soon as Santiago de Cuba was in our hands, we would immediately have readied the people for war. Bayamo was attacked precisely to situate our advance forces along the Cauto River. Never forget that this province which has a million and a half inhabitants today, provides without a doubt the best resistance and the most patriotic men of Cuba. It was this province that continued the fight for independence for thirty years and paid the highest tribute in blood, sacrifice and heroism. In Oriente, you can still breathe the air of that glorious epoch. At dawn, when the cocks crow as if they were bugles calling soldiers to reveille, and when the sun rises, radiant, over the rugged mountains, it seems that once again we will hear the cry of Yara or Baire.[1]

I stated that the second consideration on which we based our chances for success was one of social order because we were assured of the people's support. When we speak of the people we do not mean the comfortable ones, the conservative elements of the nation, who welcome any regime of oppression, any dictatorship, any despotism, prostrating themselves before the master of

[1]"Yara" on October 10, 1868, was the first battlecry for independence. The cry of "Baire" on February 24, 1895, announced the final drive to liberate Cuba from Spanish rule.

the moment until they grind their foreheads into the ground. When we speak of struggle, the *people* means the vast unredeemed masses, to whom all make promises and whom all deceive; we mean the people who yearn for a better, more dignified and more just nation; who are moved by ancestral aspirations of justice, for they have suffered injustice and mockery, generation after generation; who long for great and wise changes in all aspects of their life; people, who, to attain these changes, are ready to give even the very last breath of their lives—when they believe in something or in someone, especially when they believe in themselves. In stating a purpose, the first condition of sincerity and good faith, is to do precisely what nobody else ever does, that is, to speak with absolute clarity, without fear. The demagogues and professional politicians who manage to perform the miracle of being right in everything and in pleasing everyone, are, of necessity, deceiving everyone about everything. The revolutionaries must proclaim their ideas courageously, define their principles and express their intentions so that no one is deceived, neither friend nor foe.

The people we counted on in our struggle were these:

Seven hundred thousand Cubans without work, who desire to earn their daily bread honestly without having to emigrate in search of livelihood.

Five hundred thousand farm laborers inhabiting miserable shacks, who work four months of the year and starve for the rest of the year, sharing their misery with their children, who have not an inch of land to cultivate, and whose existence inspires compassion in any heart not made of stone.

Four hundred thousand industrial laborers and ste-
vedores whose retirement funds have been embezzled,
whose benefits are being taken away, whose homes are
wretched quarters, whose salaries pass from the hands of
the boss to those of the usurer, whose future is a pay re-
duction and dismissal, whose life is eternal work and
whose only rest is in the tomb.

One hundred thousand small farmers who live and
die working on land that is not theirs, looking at it with
sadness as Moses did the promised land, to die without
possessing it; who, like feudal serfs, have to pay for the
use of their parcel of land by giving up a portion of their
products; who cannot love it, improve it, beautify it or
plant a lemon or an orange tree on it, because they never
know when a sheriff will come with the rural guard to
evict them from it.

Thirty thousand teachers and professors who are so
devoted, dedicated and necessary to the better destiny
of future generations and who are so badly treated and
paid.

Twenty thousand small business men weighted
down by debts, ruined by the crisis and harangued by a
plague of filibusters and venal officials.

Ten thousand young professionals: doctors, engi-
neers, lawyers, veterinarians, school teachers, dentists,
pharmacists, newspapermen, painters, sculptors, etc.,
who come forth from school with their degrees, anxious
to work and full of hope, only to find themselves at a
dead end with all doors closed, and where no ear hears
their clamor or supplication.

These are the people, the ones who know misfortune and, therefore, are capable of fighting with limitless
courage!

To the people whose desperate roads through life have been paved with the brick of betrayals and false promises, we were not going to say: "we will eventually give you what you need, but rather—Here you have it, fight for it with all your might so that liberty and happiness may be yours!"

12

In the brief of this cause there must be recorded the five revolutionary laws that would have been proclaimed immediately after the capture of the Moncada barracks and would have been broadcast to the nation by radio. It is possible that Colonel Chaviano may deliberately have destroyed these documents, but even if he has done so, I conserve them in my memory.

The First Revolutionary Law would have returned power to the people and proclaimed the Constitution of 1940 the supreme Law of the land, until such time as the people should decide to modify or change it. And, in order to effect its implementation and punish those who had violated it—there being no organization for holding elections to accomplish this—the revolutionary movement, as the momentous incarnation of this sovereignty, the only source of legitimate power, would have assumed all the faculties inherent to it, except that of modifying the Constitution itself: In other words it would have assumed the legislative, executive and judicial powers.

This approach could not be more crystal clear nor

more free of vacillation and sterile charlatanry. A government acclaimed by the mass of rebel people would be vested with every power, everything necessary in order to proceed with the effective implementation of the popular will and true justice. From that moment, the Judicial Power, which since March 10th has placed itself *against* the Constitution and *outside* the Constitution, would cease to exist and we would proceed to its immediate and total reform before it would again assume the power granted to it by the Supreme Law of the Republic. Without our first taking those previous measures, a return to legality by putting the custody of the courts back into the hands that have crippled the system so dishonorably would constitute a fraud, a deceit, and one more betrayal.

The Second Revolutionary Law would have granted property, not mortgageable and not transferable, to all planters, sub-planters, lessees, partners and squatters who hold parcels of five or less "caballerias"[1] of land, and the state would indemnify the former owners on the basis of the rental which they would have received for these parcels over a period of ten years.

The Third Revolutionary Law would have granted workers and employees the right to share 30% of the profits of all the large industrial, mercantile and mining enterprises, including the sugar mills. The strictly agricultural enterprises would be exempt in consideration of other agrarian laws which would have been implemented.

The Fourth Revolutionary Law would have granted all planters the right to share 55% of the sugar produc-

[1]Tract of land, about 33⅓ acres.

tion and a minimum quota of forty thousand "arrobas"[2] for all small planters who have been established for three or more years.

The Fifth Revolutionary Law would have ordered the confiscation of all holdings and ill-gotten gains of those who had committed frauds during previous regimes, as well as the holdings and ill-gotten gains of all their legatees and heirs. To implement this, special courts with full powers would gain access to all records of all corporations registered or operating in this country [in order] to investigate concealed funds of illegal origin, and to request that foreign governments extradite persons and attach holdings [rightfully belonging to the Cuban people]. Half of the property recovered would be used to subsidize retirement funds for workers and the other half would be used for hospitals, asylums and charitable organizations.

Furthermore, it was to be declared that the Cuban policy in the Americas would be one of close solidarity with the democratic people of this continent, and that those politically persecuted by bloody tyrants oppressing our sister nations would find generous asylum, brotherhood, and bread in the land of Marti. Not the persecution, hunger and treason that they find today. Cuba should be the bulwark of liberty and not a shameful link in the chain of despotism.

[2]An *arroba* is 25 pounds.

13

These laws would have been proclaimed immediately, as soon as the upheaval were ended and prior to a detailed and far-reaching study, they would have been followed by another series of laws and fundamental measures, such as, the Agrarian Reform, Integral Reform of Education, nationalization of the Utilities Trust and the Telephone Trust, refund to the people of the illegal excessive rates this company has charged, and payment to the Treasury of all taxes brazenly evaded in the past.

All these laws and others would be inspired in the exact fulfillment of two essential articles of our Constitution. One of these orders the outlawing of feudal estates by indicating the maximum area of land any person or entity can possess for each type of agricultural enterprise, by adopting measures which would tend to revert the land to the Cubans. The other categorically orders the State to use all means at its disposal to provide employment to all those who lack it and to insure a decent livelihood to each manual laborer or intellectual.

None of these articles may be called unconstitutional. The first popularly elected government would have to respect these laws, not only because of moral obligation to the nation, but because when people achieve something they have yearned for throughout generations, no force in the world is capable of taking it away again.

The problems concerning land, the problem of industrialization, the problem of housing, the problem of unemployment, the problem of education and the problem of the health of the people; these are the six problems we would take immediate steps to resolve, along with the restoration of public liberties and political democracy.

Perhaps this exposition appears cold and theoretical if one does not know the shocking and tragic conditions of the country with regard to these six problems, to say nothing of the most humiliating political oppression.

85% of the small farmers in Cuba pay rent and live under the constant threat of being dispossessed from the land that they cultivate. More than half the best cultivated land belongs to foreigners. In *Oriente*, the largest province, the lands of the United Fruit Company and West Indian Company join the north coast to the southern one. There are two hundred thousand peasant families who do not have a single acre of land to cultivate to provide food for their starving children. On the other hand, nearly three hundred thousand "caballerias" of productive land owned by powerful interests remains uncultivated.

Cuba is above all an agricultural state. Its population is largely rural. The city depends on these rural areas. The rural people won the Independence. The greatness and prosperity of our country depends on a healthy and vigorous rural population that loves the land and knows how to cultivate it, within the framework of a state that protects and guides them. Considering all this, how can the present state of affairs be tolerated any longer?

14

With the exception of a few food, lumber and textile industries, Cuba continues to be a producer of raw materials. We export sugar to import candy, we export hides to import shoes, we export iron to import plows. Everybody agrees that the need to industrialize the country is urgent, that we need steel industries, paper and chemical industries; that we must improve cattle and grain products, the technique and the processing in our food industry, in order to balance the ruinous competition of the Europeans in cheese products, condensed milk, liquors and oil, and that of the Americans in canned goods; that we need merchant ships; that tourism should be an enormous source of revenue. But the capitalists insist that the workers remain under a Claudian[1] yoke; the State folds its arms and industrialization can wait for the Greek calends.

Just as serious or even worse is the housing problem. There are two hundred thousand huts and hovels in Cuba; four hundred thousand families in the country and in the cities live cramped into barracks and tenements without even the minimum sanitary requirements; two million two hundred thousand of our urban population pay rents which absorb between one fifth and one third of their income; and two million eight hundred thousand of our rural and suburban population lack electricity. If the State proposes lowering rents, landlords threaten to freeze all construction; if the State does not interfere, construction goes on so long as the landlords get high rents, otherwise, they would not lay a single brick even

[1]Refers to Roman Emperor Claudius Caecus who so oppressed the plebians that they left Rome.

57

though the rest of the population should have to live exposed to the elements. The utilities monopoly is no better: they extend lines as far as it is profitable and beyond that point, they don't care if the people have to live in darkness for the rest of their lives. The State folds its arms and the people have neither homes nor electricity.

Our educational system is perfectly compatible with the rest of our national situation. Where the *guajiro*[2] is not the owner of his land, what need is there for agricultural schools? Where there are no industries what need is there for technical or industrial schools? Everything falls within the same absurd logic: there is neither one thing nor the other. In any small European country there are more than 200 technical and industrial arts schools; in Cuba, there are only six such schools, and the boys graduate without having anywhere to use their skills. The little rural schools are attended by only half the school-age children—barefoot, half-naked and undernourished—and frequently the teacher must buy necessary materials from his own salary. Is this the way to make a nation great?

15

Only death can liberate one from so much misery. In this, however,—early death—the state is most helpful. 90% of rural children are consumed by parasites

---

[2]Term usually refers to modest and underprivileged farmers in Oriente province.

which filter through their bare feet from the earth. Society is moved to compassion upon hearing of the kidnapping or murder of one child, but they are criminally indifferent to the mass murder of so many thousands of children who die every year from lack of facilities, agonizing with pain. Their innocent eyes—death already shining in them—seem to look into infinity as if entreating forgiveness for human selfishness, as if asking God to stay his wrath. When the head of a family works only four months a year, with what can he purchase clothing and medicine for his children? They will grow up with rickets, with not a single good tooth in their mouths by the time they reach thirty; they will have heard ten million speeches and will finally die of misery and deception. Public hospitals, which are always full, accept only patients recommended by some powerful politician who, in turn, demands the electoral votes of the unfortunate one and his family so that Cuba may continue forever the same or worse.

With this background, is it not understandable that from May to December over a million persons lost their jobs, and that Cuba, with a population of five and a half million, has a greater percentage of unemployed than France or Italy with a population of forty million each?

When you judge a defendant for robbery, Your Honors, do you ask him how long he has been unemployed? Do you ask him how many children he has, which days of the week he ate and which he didn't, do you concern yourselves with his environment at all? You send him to jail without further thought. But those who burn warehouses and stores to collect insurance do not go to jail, even though a few human beings should have happened to [be cremated with the property insured].

The insured have money to hire lawyers and bribe judges. You jail the poor wretch who steals because he is hungry; but none of the hundreds who steal from the Government has ever spent a night in jail; you dine with them at the end of the year in some elegant place and they enjoy your respect.

In Cuba when a bureaucrat becomes a millionaire overnight and enters the fraternity of the rich, he could very well be greeted with the words of that opulent Balzac character, Taillefer, who, in his toast to the young heir to an enormous fortune, said: "Gentlemen, let us drink to the power of gold! Mr. Valentine, a millionaire six time over has just ascended the throne. He is king, can do everything, is above everything—like all the rich. Henceforward, equality before the law, before the Constitution, will be a myth for him; for he will not be subject to laws, the laws will be subject to him. There are no courts or sentences for millionaires."

The future of the country and the solution of its problems cannot continue to depend on the selfish interests of a dozen financiers, nor on the cold calculations of profits that ten or twelve magnates draw up in their air-conditioned offices. The country cannot continue begging on its knees for miracles from a few golden calves, similar to the Biblical one destroyed by the fury of a prophet. Golden calves cannot perform miracles of any kind. The problems of the Republic can be solved only if we dedicate ourselves to fight for that Republic with the same energy, honesty and patriotism our liberators had when they created it.

16

It is not by statesmen such as Carlos Saladrigas,[1] whose statesmanship consists of preserving the status quo and mouthing phrases like the "absolute freedom of enterprise," "guarantees to investment capital" and "the law of supply and demand," that we will solve these problems. Those ministers can chat gaily in a mansion on Fifth Avenue[2] until there remains not even the dust of the bones of those whose problems required immediate solution. In this present-day world, social problems are not solved by spontaneous generation.

A revolutionary government with the backing of the people and the respect of the nation, after cleaning the various institutions of all venal and corrupt officials, would proceed immediately to industrialize the country, mobilizing all inactive capital, currently estimated at about 500 million dollars, through the National Bank and the Agricultural, Industrial and Development Bank, and submitting this mammoth task to experts and men of absolute competence, completely removed from all political machinations, for study, direction, planning and realization.

After settling the one hundred thousand small farmers as owners on land which they previously rented, a revolutionary government would proceed immediately to settle the land problem. First, as the Constitution orders we would establish the maximum amount of land to be held by each type of agricultural enterprise and would acquire the excess acres by: expropriation, recov-

[1]Batista's presidential candidate in 1944 elections, Saladrigas was defeated.
[2]Located in Miramar residential district of Havana.

61

ery of the lands stolen from the State, improvement of swampland, planting of large nurseries and reserving of zones for reforestation. Secondly, we would distribute the remaining land among peasant families with priority given to the larger ones, and would promote agricultural cooperatives with a single technical, professional direction in farming and cattle raising. Finally, we would provide resources, equipment, protection and useful guidance to the peasants.

A revolutionary government would solve the housing problem by cutting all rents in half, by providing tax exemptions on homes inhabited by the owners; by tripling taxes on rented homes; by tearing down hovels and replacing them with modern multiple-dwelling buildings; and by financing housing all over the island on a scale heretofore unheard of; with the criterion that, just as each rural family should possess its own tract of land, each city family should own its home or apartment. There is plenty of building material and more than enough manpower to make a decent home for every Cuban. But if we continue to wait for the miracle of the golden calf, a thousand years will have gone by and the problem will still be the same. On the other hand, today there are greater than ever possibilities of bringing electricity to the remotest corner of the island. The use of nuclear energy in this field is now a reality and will greatly reduce the cost of producing electricity.

With these three projects and reforms, the problem of unemployment would automatically disappear and the work to improve public health and to fight against disease would be made much less difficult.

Finally, a revolutionary government would undertake the integral reform of the educational system, bringing it in line with the foregoing projects with the idea of educating those generations who will have the privilege of living in a happy land. Do not forget the words of the Apóstol:[3] "A serious error is being made in Latin America: where the inhabitants depend almost exclusively on the products of the soil for their livelihood, the education stress, contradictorally, is on urban rather than farm life." "The happiest people are the ones whose children are well-educated and instructed in philosophy; whose sentiments are directed into noble channels." "A well-educated people will always be strong and free."

The spirit of education lies, however, in the teacher himself and in Cuba the teaching profession is miserably underpaid. Despite this, no one is more dedicated than the Cuban teacher. Who among us has not learned his ABC's in the little public schoolhouse? It is time we stopped paying pittances to these young men and women who are entrusted with the sacred task of teaching the young. No teacher should earn less than $200, no secondary professor should get less than $350, if they are to devote themselves exclusively to their high calling without suffering want. Moreover, all rural teachers should have free use of the various systems of transportation; and, at least every five years, all teachers should enjoy a sabbatical leave of six months with pay so they may attend special refresher courses at home and abroad to keep abreast of the latest developments in their field. In this way, the curriculum and the teaching system may be constantly improved.

Where will the money be found for all this? When there is an end to rife embezzlement of government

[3]Refers to Jose Martí.

funds, when public officials stop taking graft from the large companies who owe taxes to the State, when the enormous resources of the country are brought into full use, when we no longer buy tanks, bombers and guns for this country (which has no frontiers to defend and where these instruments of war, now being purchased, are used against the people) when there is more interest in educating the people than in killing them—then there will be more than enough money.

17

Cuba could easily provide for a population three times as great as it now has, so there is no excuse for the abject poverty of a single one of its present inhabitants. The markets should be overflowing with produce, pantries should be full, all hands should be working. This is not an inconceivable thought. What is inconceivable is that anyone should go to bed hungry, that children should die for lack of medical attention; what is inconceivable is that 30% of our farm people cannot write their names and that 99% of them know nothing of Cuba's history. What is inconceivable is that the majority of our rural people are now living in worse circumstances than were the Indians Columbus discovered living in the fairest land that human eyes had ever seen.

To those who would call me a dreamer, I quote the words of Marti: "A true man does not seek the path where advantage lies, but rather, the path where duty lies, and this is the only practical man, whose dream of today will be the law of tomorrow, because he who has looked back on the upheavals of history and has seen civilizations going up in flames, crying out in bloody struggle, throughout the centuries, knows that the future well-being of man, without exception, lies on the side of duty."

18

Only when we understand that such high ideals inspired them, can we conceive of the heroism of the young men who fell in Santiago.

The meager material means at our disposal was all that prevented our certain success. When the soldiers were told that Prío[1] had given a million dollars to us, they were told this in the regime's attempt to distort the most serious fact—the fact that our movement had no link with past politicians. The regime [was trying] to prevent the soldiers from learning that this movement is a new Cuban generation with its own ideas, rising up against tyranny; that this movement is made up of young men who were barely seven years old when Batista committed the first of his crimes in 1934.

The lie about the million dollars could not have been more absurd. If, with less than $20,000, we armed 165 men and attacked one regiment and one squadron,

[1]Participated in overthrow of Machado, later becoming member of Grau San Martin's cabinet, finally was elected President of Cuba in 1948.

then with a million dollars we could have armed 8,000 men to attack fifty regiments and fifty squadrons—and Ugalde Carrillo[2] would not have found out until Sunday, July 26th, at 5:15 A.M. I assure you that for every man who fought, twenty well-trained men were unable to fight, for lack of arms. When these men paraded along the streets of Havana with the student demonstration on the Centenary of Marti, they solidly packed six city blocks. If even 200 more men had been able to fight [at Moncada] or had we possessed 20 more hand-grenades, perhaps this honorable court would have been spared all this bother.

The politicians spent millions of dollars buying off consciences, whereas, a handful of Cubans who wanted to save their country's honor, had to face death—barehanded, for lack of funds. This explains why the country, to this very day, has been governed not by generous and dedicated men, but by political racketeers, the scum of our public life.

With pride, therefore, I say that, in accord with our principles, we have asked no past or present politician for a penny. Those who gave us funds for the cause did so with sacrifice beyond compare. For example, Elpidio Sosa who gave up his job and came to me one day with $300 for the cause; Fernando Chenard, who sold the photographic equipment with which he earned his livelihood; Pedro Marrero, who contributed several months' salary and who had to be stopped from actually selling the very furniture in his house; Oscar Alcalde, who sold his pharmaceutical laboratory, and Jesús Mon-

[2]Colonel Ugalde Carrillo, Commander of Batista's armed forces in the region neighboring the town of Nicaro.

tané, who gave his five years' savings, and so on, with many others each giving the little he had.

One must have great faith in his country to do such a thing. The remembrance of these gestures of idealism brings me straight to the most bitter chapter of this defense—the price that tyranny made them pay for wanting to free Cuba from oppression and injustice.

19

Multiply by ten the crimes of November 27th, 1871,[1] and you will have the monstrous and repulsive crimes of the 26th, 27th, 28th, and 29th of July, 1953, in Oriente Province. These are still fresh in our memory, but someday after years have passed by, when the skies of this nation are clear once again, when tempers are calmed and fear no longer torments our spirits, then we will begin to see the magnitude of the massacre in all of its shocking reality. And future generations will be struck with horror whenever they look back on these acts of barbarity unprecedented in our history. But I do not want to become enraged. I need clearness of mind and peace in my heavy heart, in order to relate the deeds as simply as possible, in no sense dramatizing them, but just as they took place. I feel shame as a Cuban that heartless men should have committed such unthinkable

[1]When a group of medical students were summarily executed for supposedly desecrating the grave of a Spanish grandee.

crimes, dishonoring our country before the rest of the world.

This tyrant Batista was never a man of scruples. He has never hesitated to tell his people the most outrageous lies. To justify his coup of the 10th of March, he concocted stories about a fictitious army uprising, which was supposedly scheduled to occur in April, and which he "wanted to avert so that the Republic might not be drenched in blood." A ridiculous little tale nobody believed! And when he himself *did* want to drench the Republic in blood, when he wanted to smother in terror and torture the [rightful and] just rebellion of Cuba's youth, who were not willing to be his slaves, then he contrived still more fantastic lies. What little respect one must have for a people when one tries to deceive them so miserably!

20

On the very day of my arrest I publicly assumed responsibility for our armed movement on the 26th of July. If there had been an iota of truth in even one of the many statements the Dictator made against our fighters, in his speech on July 27th, that would have been enough to undermine the moral impact of my case. Why then, was I not brought to trial? Why were medical certificates forged? Why did [the regime] violate all laws during the proceedings and desecrate so scandalously the rulings of the Court? Why were so many things done—things never before seen done in a court of law—in order to prevent my appearance at all costs? In contrast I could not begin to tell you all I went through in order to appear. I asked the Court to bring me to trial in accordance with all established principles, and I denounced the underhanded schemes that were afoot to prevent it. I wanted to argue with [my accusers] face to face.

But they did *not* wish to [face me]. Who was telling the truth and who was not? The declarations made by the Dictator at Camp Columbia could be considered amusing if so many lives were not involved.

He claimed we were a group of hirelings and that amongst us were many foreigners. He said that the central part of our plan was an attempt to kill him—him, him, always him. As if the men who attacked Camp Moncada could not have killed him and twenty like him, had they approved of [private assassination] tactics.

He stated that our attack had been planned by ex-president Prío—and that it had been financed with Prío's money. It has been proved irrefutably that there existed no link whatsoever between our movement and the last regime.

He claimed that we had machine guns and hand grenades. Yet the military technicians have stated right here that we had only one machine gun and not a single hand-grenade.

He said that we had beheaded the sentries. Yet death certificates and medical reports of all the army's casualties show no deaths were caused by the blade.

But, above all—and most important—he said that we stabbed patients at the Military Hospital. Yet the doctors of that hospital—mind you, Army doctors—have testified we never even occupied *that* building, that no patient was either wounded *or* killed by us, and that the hospital lost only one employee—a janitor who imprudently put his head out an open window.

21

Whenever a Chief of State—or anybody pretending to be one—makes declarations to the country, he speaks not just to hear the sound of his own voice. He always has some specific motive and expects some specific reaction. Since we had already been defeated militarily, inasmuch as we no longer represented any actual danger to the dictatorship, why did they slander us in such a fashion? If it is still not clear that his speech was just an attempt to justify the crimes that they had been committing since the night before—and which they were going to continue committing—then, let the numbers speak for me.

On the 27th of July, in his speech from the military headquarters, Batista said that the assailants suffered thirty-three dead. At the end of the week, the number of dead had risen to more than eighty men. In what battles, in what places, in what clashes, did these young men die? Before Batista spoke, more than twenty-five prisoners had been murdered. After Batista spoke, fifty more were murdered.

What a great sense of honor was shown by those soldiers and officers, who did not distort the facts before the court but gave their reports adhering to the strictest

70

truth. These surely are soldiers who honor the uniform, and these, surely, are men! Neither a real soldier nor a true man can degrade his code of living with lies and crime.

I know that many of the soldiers are indignant at the barbaric assassinations committed. I know that they feel repugnance and shame at the smell of homicidal blood that impregnates every stone of Camp Moncada.

Now that he has been contradicted by men of honor among his own army, I defy the dictator to repeat his vile slander against us. I defy him to try to justify before the Cuban people, his speech of the 27th of July.

Let him not be quiet. Let him speak. Let him say who are the assassins, the ruthless, the inhumane. Let him tell us if the medals of honor, which he went to pin on the breasts of his heroes of the massacre, were reward for the hideous crimes they had committed. Let him, from this very moment, assume his responsibility before history. Let him not pretend, at a later date, that the soldiers were acting without orders from him! Let him offer the nation an explanation for these seventy murders. There was a lot of bloodshed. The nation needs an explanation. The nation demands it.

It was common knowledge that in 1933, at the end of the battle at the Hotel Nacional, some officers were murdered after surrendering; Bohemia Magazine protested energetically. It was known too that after the surrender of Fort Atarés, the besiegers' machine guns cut down a row of prisoners. And that one soldier, demanding "Who is Blas Hernández?[1]" then blasted Blas

[1]Officer of the Atarés regiment who was shot in the act of surrendering.

Hernández with a bullet directly in the face—and for this cowardly act was promoted to officer's rank.

It was well known in Cuban history that assassination of prisoners was fatally linked with the name of Batista. Such naiveté on our part [not to foresee what would happen]. However—unjustifiable as those acts were in 1933—they happened in a matter of minutes, in no more time than it took for a round of machine gun fire. Furthermore they happened while combat nerves were still on edge. It was not thus in Santiago de Cuba. Here all forms of vicious abuse were [deliberately] overdone.

Our men were killed not in the course of a minute, an hour or a day. Throughout a whole week the blows, the torture, and the shots continued, ceasing not for an instant—as methods of grisly amusement—wielded by well-practiced artisans of crime. Camp Moncada was converted into a workshop of torture and death. And some base individuals exchanged their uniforms for butchers aprons. The walls were splattered with blood. The bullets imbedded in the walls were encrusted with singed bits of skin, brains and human hair—the grisly reminders of rifle shots full in the face. The grass around the barracks was dark and sticky with human blood. The criminal hands that are guiding the destiny of Cuba had written for the prisoners at the entrance of that den of death the very inscription of Hell: "Abandon all hope."

22

They did not even attempt to disguise appearances. They did not bother in the least to conceal what they were doing. They thought they had deceived the people with their lies and they ended deceiving themselves. They felt themselves lords and masters of the universe, with power over life and death. So the fear they had experienced upon our attack at daybreak was dissipated in an orgy of cadavers—they were truly drunk with blood.

Chronicles of our history, down through four and a half centuries, tell us of many acts of cruelty—the slaughter of defenseless Indians by the Spaniards; the plundering and atrocities of pirates along the coast; the barbarities of the Spanish soldiers during the War of Independence; the shooting of prisoners of the Cuban army by the forces of Weyler; the horrors of the Machado regime—and so on to the crimes of March 1935. But with none was there written a page so bloody, so sad—in the number of victims and in the viciousness of those who victimized—as in Santiago de Cuba eleven weeks ago.

Only one man in all these centuries has stained with blood two separate periods of our historic existence and has dug his claws into the flesh of two generations of Cubans. To release this river of blood, he waited for the Centenary[1] of the *Apostol*, and the fiftieth anniversary of the Republic, [whose people gained] freedom, human rights, and happiness by the forfeit of so many lives. Even greater is his crime and even more to be condemned because the man who committed it had already,

[1] By dramatic coincidence, 1953 was the 100th anniversary of Marti's birth and the fiftieth anniversary of Cuba's independence.

for eleven long years, lorded over this people—this people who, by such deep-rooted sentiment and tradition, adore freedom and repudiate evil. This man has furthermore never been sincere, loyal, honest or chivalrous for a single minute of his public life. He was not content with the treachery of December 1933,[2] the crimes of March 1935 and the forty million dollar fortune that crowned his first regime; he had to add the treason of March 1952, the crimes of July 1953 and a hoard of millions that only time will tell.

Dante divided his hell into nine levels. He put in the seventh the criminals, in the eighth the thieves, and in the ninth the traitors. Difficult dilemma the devils would be faced with, endeavoring to find an adequate destination for the soul of this man—if this man had a soul. The man who encouraged the atrocious acts in Santiago de Cuba has not even human entrails. I heard many details from the lips of some soldiers, full of shame, who recounted to me the wicked scenes they had witnessed.

23

As soon as the fighting was over, the soldiers descended like savage beasts over the city of Santiago. And they indulged their first fury against the defenseless pop-

[2]When Batista realized that Grau San Martin, whom he had placed in power in September, 1933, would be unable to procure recognition from the United States, he maneuvered a switch of military support and precipitated Grau's resignation in January, 1934.

ulation. In the middle of the street, far from the site where the fighting had taken place, they fired a bullet through the chest of an innocent child, as he was at play beside his doorstep. And when the father approached, to pick him up, they shot him through the forehead with another bullet. Without a word they shot "Nino" Cala, who was on his way home with a loaf of bread in his hands. It would be an endless task to relate all the crimes and outrages committed against the civil population.

When the Army dealt that way with those who had had no part in the action, you can imagine the terrible fate of the prisoners who *had* taken part in the action—or whom they believed to have taken part. Just as, in this trial, they *accused* many people not at all involved in our attack, they also *killed* many prisoners who had not been involved in the attack. The latter are not included in the statistics of victims the regime has given out; those statistics refer exclusively to our own men. Someday the total number of annihilated will be known.

24

The first prisoner killed was our medico. Dr. Mario Muñoz, who bore no arms, wore no uniform and was dressed in the white smock of Galen. He was a man generous and able, who would have given to the wounded adversary the same devoted care as to a friend. On the road from the City Hospital to the Camp, they shot him in the back and left him lying there, face downward in a pool of blood. But the mass murder of prisoners did not begin until after three o'clock in the afternoon. Until this hour they awaited orders.

Then General Martín Díaz Tamayo arrived from Havana and brought specific instructions from a meeting which he had attended with Batista, along with the head of the army, the head of the Military Intelligence Service, and others. He said: "It is humiliating and dishonorable for the army to have lost in combat three times as many men as the insurgents did. Ten prisoners must be killed for each dead soldier." This was the order.

In every society there are found men of base instincts. These sadists—brutes, conveyors of all the ancestral atavisms—go about in the guise of human beings, but they are monsters only more or less restrained by discipline and social habit. If they are offered a drink from a river of blood, they will not be satisfied until they drink the river dry.

What these men needed precisely was this order. At their hands the best and noblest of Cuba perished; the most valiant, the most honest, the most idealistic. The tyrant called them mercenaries. There they were dying as heroes at the hands of men who collect a salary from the Republic, and who, with the arms which the Republic gave them to defend her, serve the interests of a mob and murder the best of her citizens.

25

Throughout their torturing of our comrades the Army offered them a chance to save their lives by betraying their ideologic position and falsely declaring that Prío had given them money. When they indignantly rejected that proposition, the Army continued torturing them horribly. They shattered their testicles and they tore out their eyes. But no one yielded. And no complaint or begging was heard. Even when they had been deprived of their virile organs, our boys were still a thousand times more manly than all their tormentors together. Photographs—which do not lie—show the bodies to have been dismembered.

Other methods were employed. Frustrated by the valour of the men, they tried to break the spirit of the women. With a bleeding human eye in his hands, a sergeant and several other men went to the cell where our comrades Melba Hernández and Haydée Santamaría were held. Addressing the latter and showing her the eye, they said: "This eye belonged to your brother. If you will not testify what he refused to testify we will tear out the other." She, who loved her valiant brother above all things, replied, full of dignity: "If you tore out an eye and he did not testify falsely, much less will I."

Later they came back and burned her arms with lit cigarettes until at last full of disrespect they told her: You no longer have a fiancé because we have killed him too. But, imperturbable, she answered: "He is not dead; to die for your country is to live on."

Never has there been placed on so high a pedestal the heroism and the dignity of Cuban womanhood.

26

There was no respect even for combat-wounded in the various hospitals in the city, where they were hunted down as a prey is pursued by a vulture. In the Centro Gallego they broke into the operating room at the very instant when two of our critically wounded were receiving blood transfusions. They yanked them off the tables and, as the wounded could not remain upright, they dragged them down to the basement where they arrived as corpses.

They could not do the same in the Spanish Colony, where Gustavo Arcos and José Ponce were patients, because they were prevented by Dr. Posada who bravely told them they could enter only over his dead body.

Air and camphor were injected into the veins of Pedro Miret, Abelardo Crespo and Fidel Labrador, in an attempt to kill them, in the Military Hospital. They owe their lives to Captain Tamayo, an army doctor, and a true soldier of honor who, with pistol in hand, wrenched them out of their merciless captors' grasp and transferred them to the City Hospital. These five young men were the only ones of our wounded to survive.

In the early morning hours groups of our men were removed from the garrison. They were taken in automobiles to Siboney, La Maya, Songo and elsewhere. Then they were led out—tied, gagged and already disfigured by torture—and were murdered in these out-of-the-way places. They are recorded as having perished in combat against the army. After several days of this procedure, few of the captured prisoners survived.

Many were compelled to dig their own graves. One of our men, while he performed this operation, wheeled around and marked the face of one of his assassins with his pick. Others of our men were buried alive, their hands tied behind their backs.

Many solitary spots have become the graveyards of the brave. On the army target range alone, five of our men lie buried. Someday these men will be disinterred. Then they will be carried on the shoulders of the people to a monument which, alongside the tomb of Martí, their liberated land will surely erect to honor the memory of the Martyrs of the Centenary.

27

The last youth assassinated in the region of Santiago de Cuba was Mario Martí. With our colleague Ciro Redondo, he was captured in a cave at Siboney on the morning of Thursday the 30th. As these two men, arms upraised, were led down the road, the soldiers shot Mario Martí in the back and after he had fallen to the ground, riddled him with bullets. Redondo was taken to the camp. When Mayor Pérez Chaumont saw him, he exclaimed: "And this one—why have you brought *him* to me?" The court was able to hear the narration of this incident from the lips of the young man who had survived thanks to what Pérez Chaumont called "the stupidity of the soldiers."

The order was the same throughout the whole province. Ten days after July 26th a newspaper of this city printed the news that two youths had been found hanged on the road from Manzanillo to Bayamo. Later they were identified as the bodies of Hugo Camejo and Pedro Vélez. Another extraordinary incident had taken place there. The victims had been three, removed from Manzanillo barracks at two o'clock in the morning. At a certain spot on the highway, they were taken out, beaten till they were unconscious, and strangled to death with a rope. But, after they had been given up for dead, one of them—Andres García—regained consciousness and took refuge in the house of a farmer. Thanks to this, the Court could learn the details of this crime, too. Of all our men taken prisoner in the Bayamo area, this boy was the only survivor.

Near the Cauto River,[1] in a spot known as Barrancas, at the bottom of a well, lie the bodies of Raúl de Aguiar, Armando del Valle and Andrés Valdés. They were murdered at midnight on the Alto Cedro-Palma Soriano road by Sergeant Montes de Oca, head of the barracks at Miranda, Corporal Maceo, and the Lieutenant in charge of Alto Cedro, where the three murdered men were captured.

[1]The longest river in Cuba, forming a broad and fertile flood plain in Oriente Province. Many of the towns that achieved historical status both in the War of Independence and in Castro's 26th of July revolt are located in this fertile valley.

28

In the annals of evil, distinction is due to Sergeant Eulalio González, known as "the tiger" of Camp Moncada. This man felt no qualms even in bragging about his unspeakable deeds. It was he who with his own hands murdered our comrade Abel Santamaría. But, still he was not satisfied. One day as he was returning from the prison of Puerto Boniato, where he raises pedigreed fighting cocks in the backyard, he boarded a bus on which Abel's mother was travelling. When this monster realized who she was, he began referring to his grisly deeds and in a loud voice—so that the mother, dressed in mourning, could hear him—he said, "Yes, I have extracted many eyes and expect to continue extracting them." In that mother's sobs of grief at the crude and cowardly insolence of the very murderer of her son, we can find expressed beyond power of any words the unprecedented moral opprobrium our nation is suffering. When these selfsame mothers went to Camp Moncada to ask about their sons, they were given an answer unheard-of in its callousness: "Certainly, Madame, you may go see him—at Hotel Santa Efigenia,[1] where we have put him up for you." Either Cuba is not Cuba, or the men responsible for these acts will have to meet a dire day of reckoning. Heartless men, they coarsely insulted the Cuban people who uncovered their heads in reverence as the corpses of their young rebels were carried by.

So many were the victims that the government has not yet dared to make public the complete casualty lists. They know that their figures are all out of proportion.

[1]Cemetery in the province of Santiago.

They *do* have the names of all the victims, because prior to murdering every prisoner they recorded his vital statistics. The whole long process of identification through the National Cabinet[2] was pure pantomime and there are families who still await word of the fate of their sons. Now that almost three months have elapsed, why is the question still open?

I wish to confirm that the victims' pockets were probed for the very last penny and that all their personal effects, rings and watches were stripped from their bodies and are brazenly worn today by their assassins.

29

A great part of what I have just related, you already know, Honorable Magistrates, from the testimony of many of my colleagues. But please note that many key witnesses have been barred from this trial, although they were permitted to attend the other sessions of the trial. For example, I point out that the nurses of the City Hospital are absent although they work in the same building where this hearing is taking place. They were prevented from appearing so that, under my questioning, they could not testify to the fact that, besides Dr. Mario Munoz, twenty other men were captured alive here. The regime fears that from the questioning of these witnesses, some extremely dangerous testimony would get into the official trial records.

[2]Identification bureau.

But Major Perez Chaumont did appear here and he could not elude my questioning. What we learned from this man—a hero who fought only against unarmed and handcuffed men—gives us an idea of what could have been learned at the Courthouse if I had not been isolated from the proceedings. I asked him how many of our men had died in his celebrated skirmishes at Siboney. He hesitated. I insisted and he finally said twenty-one. Since I knew no such skirmishes had ever taken place, I asked him how many of our men had been wounded. He answered: none; all of them had been killed. It was then that I asked him, in astonishment, if the soldiers were using nuclear weapons. Of course, where men are shot point blank, there are no wounded.

I asked him afterwards how many casualties the Army had sustained. He replied that two of his men had been wounded. I asked him finally if neither of those two had died and he said no. I waited. Later, all of the wounded Army soldiers filed by and it was discovered that none of them had been wounded at Siboney. This same Major Perez Chaumont who hardly flinched at having assassinated twenty defenseless young men had built in Ciudamar Beach a palatial home worth more than $100,000—his savings after only a few months under Batista's new rule. And if a major has saved this much, what must the generals have saved!

30

Honorable Magistrates: Where are our boys who were captured during the 26th, 27th, 28th and 29th of July? There are known to be over sixty captured men from the area of Santiago de Cuba. Only three of them and the two girls have appeared. The rest of the accused were seized later. Where are our wounded? Only five of them are alive, the rest were murdered. The figures are irrefutable.

On the other hand, twenty soldiers who were our prisoners have been present here and according to their own words received not even an offensive word from us. Before you, also, appeared thirty soldiers who were wounded, many in the street fighting, and none was killed off by us. If the Army losses were nineteen dead and thirty wounded, how is it possible that we should have had eighty dead and five wounded? Who ever witnessed a battle with twenty-one dead and no wounded, like these extraordinary battles described by Perez Chaumont?

Here we have the casualty lists of the bitter fighting of the invasion troops of the war of 1895, both where the Cuban Army was victorious and where the Cuban Army was defeated. The Battle of Los Indios at Las Villas: twelve wounded, none dead; Battle of Mal Tiempo: four dead, twenty-three wounded; Battle of Calimete: sixteen dead, sixty-four wounded; Battle of La Palma: thirty-nine dead, eighty-eight wounded; Battle of Cacarajicara: five dead, thirteen wounded; Battle of Descanso: four dead, forty-five wounded; Battle of San Gabriel del Lombillo: two dead, eighteen wounded. In all of these the number of wounded is two times, three times and up to ten times greater than the number of dead, although in those days, no techniques of modern medicine existed to reduce the percentage of deaths. How then can we explain the fabulous proportion of sixteen deaths per wounded man, if not by the government's slaughter of the wounded in the very hospitals, just as they later assassinated the other helpless prisoners they had taken. The numbers speak out beyond rebuttal.

"It is a shame and a dishonor for the Army to have lost in combat three times as many men as the insurgents lost; we must kill ten prisoners for each dead soldier." This is the concept of honor held by the petty corporals made generals on the 10th of March. This is the code of honor they wish to impose on the National Army. False, pretended and superficial honor based on lies, hypocrisy and crime. (They know they need a mask to hide behind and they try to make) of blood a mask of honor. Who told them men lose their honor when they die fighting? Who told them the honor of an army consists of murdering the wounded and the prisoners of war?

31

In times of war armies that murder prisoners have always earned the contempt and abomination of the entire world. Such cowardice has no justification even in a case when national territory is invaded by foreign forces. In the words of a South American liberator: "Not even the strictest military obedience can convert a soldier's sword into a ruthless blade." The honorable soldier does not kill the helpless prisoner after the fight, but rather, respects him. He does not finish off a wounded man, but rather, helps him. He stands in the way of crime and if he cannot prevent it, he imitates that Spanish captain who, upon hearing the report of guns turned on students, indignantly broke his sword in two and refused to continue serving in that army.

The soldiers who murdered prisoners were not worthy of the soldiers who died. I saw many soldiers fight with courage, for example, those in the patrols that fired their machine guns against us in almost body to body combat or that sergeant who, defying death, grabbed the alarm to mobilize the barracks. Some of them live, I am happy for them; others are dead. They believed they were doing their duty and in my sight, this makes them worthy of admiration and respect. I deplore only the fact that valiant men should fall for an evil cause. When Cuba is freed, we should respect, shelter and aid the wives and sons of the courageous soldiers who perished fighting against us. They are not to be blamed for the miseries of Cuba. They are just so many more victims of this nefarious situation.

But the honor gained by the soldiers who died in battle was lost by generals who ordered prisoners to be killed after their surrender. Men who became generals overnight without ever firing a shot, men who bought their stars with high treason to their country, men who ordered the execution of prisoners taken in battles in which they did not participate; these are the generals of the 10th of March—generals who would have been unfit to drive the mules that carried equipment for the army of Antonio Maceo.

The Army suffered three times as many casualties as

86

we did. That was because our men were superbly trained, as the army men themselves testified; and because we had prepared adequate tactical measures, as the Army men themselves admitted. The Army failed to perform brilliantly; despite the millions spent for espionage by the Military Intelligence Service, they were taken totally by surprise; and their hand grenades failed to explode because they were obsolete. All this, the Army owes to generals like Martin Diaz Tamayo and colonels like Ugalde Carrillo and Alberto del Rio Chaviano.

We were not seventeen traitors infiltrated in the Army ranks, as was the case on the 10th of March. Rather we were 165 men who had crossed the length and breadth of the island to look death boldly in the face. If the Army leaders had had a notion of real military honor they would have resigned their commands instead of trying to wash away their shame and incompetence in the blood of prisoners.

32

To kill prisoners and then state that they died in combat—that is the military capacity of the generals of the 10th of March. That was the way the worst butchers of Valeriano Weyler[1] behaved in the worst days of our War of Independence.

[1]General appointed by Spain to carry out a punitive campaign against Cuba after Maceo's sensational march.

The Chronicles of War narrate the following incident:

"On the 23rd of February, officer Baldomero Acosta entered Punta Brava with some cavalry at the same time that there approached, from the opposite road, a squad of Pizarro's regiment led by a sergeant known around there as Barriguilla (Pot Belly). The insurgents exchanged a few salvos with Pizarro's men, then withdrew by the trail that leads from Punta Brava to the village of Guatao. Followed by another battalion of volunteers from Marianao who were led by Captain Calvo, Pizarro's squad marched on Guatao. As soon as their first forces entered the village they commenced their massacre—killing twelve throughout the peaceful neighborhood and taking the rest prisoners. Not yet satisfied with their outrages, in the outskirts of Guatao they carried out another barbaric execution killing one of the prisoners and horribly wounding the rest. The Marquise of Cervera, a complacent, pomp and circumstance soldier, informed Weyler of the pyrrhic victory of the Spanish soldiers; but Major Zugasti, a man of principle, denounced the incident to the government and officially called the murders perpetrated by the iniquitous Captain Calvo and Sergeant Barriguilla, an assassination of peaceful citizens.

"Weyler's intervention in this horrible incident and his delight upon learning the details of the massacre can be palpably deduced from the official dispatch that he sent to the Ministry of War concerning his cruelties. 'A small regiment organized by a Major from Marianao with forces from the garrison, fought, destroying the troops of Villanueva and Baldomero Acosta near Punta Brava, killing twenty of their men, who were handed over to the

Mayor of Guatao for burial, and taking fifteen prisoners, one of them wounded, and assuming many wounded among those who escaped. One of our men suffered critical wounds, many suffered light bruises and wounds. Weyler.'"

The only difference between Weyler's lines and those of Colonel Chaviano, detailing the victories of Major Perez Chaumont, is that Weyler announces twenty dead and Chaumont twenty-one; Weyler mentions one wounded soldier in his ranks, Chaviano mentions two; Weyler speaks of one wounded man and fifteen prisoners in the enemy ranks, Chaviano records neither wounded men nor prisoners.

Just as I admire the courage of the soldiers who died bravely, I also admire the officers who bore themselves with dignity and did not redden their hands with this blood. Many of the survivors owe their lives to the commendable conduct of officers like Lieutenant Sarria, Lieutenant Camps, Captain Tamayo and others, who were true gentlemen in their treatment of the prisoners. If men like these had not partially saved the name of the Armed Forces, today it would be more honorable to wear a dishrag than to wear an Army uniform.

33

For my dead friends, I claim no vengeance. Since their lives were priceless, the murderers could not pay for them with their own lives. It is not by blood that we can redeem the lives of those who died for their country.

The happiness of their people is the only tribute worthy of them.

My comrades, furthermore, are neither dead nor forgotten; they live today, more than ever, and their murderers will view with dismay the immortality of the victorious spirit of their ideas. Let the *Apóstol* speak for me:

"There is a limit to the tears we can shed at the tombs of the dead. Instead of crying over their bodies, we should go there to contemplate their infinite love for their country and its glory—a love that never hesitates, loses hope nor weakens. For the graves of the martyrs are the most beautiful altars of our day.

"When one dies
In the arms of a grateful fatherland
Death ends, prison walls break—
Finally, with death, life begins."

34

Up to this point I have confined myself almost exclusively to relating events. Since I am well aware that I am before a court convened to judge me, I will now demonstrate that all legal right was on our side alone, and that the verdict imposed on my comrades—the verdict now being sought against me—has no justification by reason, nor before society and true justice.

I wish to be duly respectful to the Honorable Magistrates and I am grateful that you find in the frankness of my plea no animosity towards you. My argument is meant merely to demonstrate what a false and erroneous position the Judicial System has adopted in the present situation.

To a certain extent, each court is nothing more than a cog in the wheel of this system and therefore, must move along the course determined by the vehicle—although, by no means, does this justify any individual to act against his principles. I know very well that the oligarchy are most to be blamed. The oligarchy, without dignified protest, abjectly yielded to the dictates of the usurper, and betrayed their country by renouncing the autonomy of the Judicial System.

Men who constitute noble exceptions have attempted to mend the system's mangled honor with their individual decisions. But the gestures of this minority have been of little consequence, drowned as they were by the obsequious and fawning majority. Although I am aware of this, it will not stop me, nevertheless, from speaking the truth that supports my cause.

My appearance before this court may be a pure farce to give the semblance of legality to arbitrary decisions, but I am determined to tear down with a firm hand the infamous veil that hides so much shamelessness. It is curious: the very men who have brought me here to be judged and condemned have never heeded a single decision of this court.

Since this trial may, as you have said, be the most important to have taken place since we achieved national sovereignty, what I say here will perhaps be lost in the silence which the dictatorship has tried to impose on me, but posterity will often turn its eyes to what you do here.

Remember that today you are judging an accused man, but that you yourselves will be judged not once, but many times—as often as these days are submitted to criticism in the future. What I say here will be repeated many times, not because it comes from my lips, but because the problem of justice is eternal and the people have a deep sense of justice, above and beyond the hair-splitting of jurisprudence. The people wield simple but implacable logic, in conflict with all that is absurd and contradictory.

Furthermore, if there is a people in the world that with all its might abhors favoritism and inequality, it is the Cuban people. To them justice is symbolized by a maiden with a scale and a sword in her hands. Should she cower before one group and furiously wield that sword against another group, then, to the people of Cuba, the maiden of justice will seem nothing more than a prostitute brandishing a dagger. My logic is the simple logic of the people.

35

Let me tell you a story.

Once upon a time there was a Republic. It had its constitution, its laws, its civil rights, a president, a Congress, and law courts. Everyone could assemble, associate, speak and write with complete freedom.

The people were not satisfied with the government officials at that time, but [the people] had the power to elect new officials and only a few days remained before they were going to do so!

There existed a public opinion both respected and

heeded and all problems of common interest were freely discussed. There were political parties, radio and television debates and forums, and public meetings. The whole nation throbbed with enthusiasm. This country had suffered greatly and although it was unhappy, it longed to be happy and had a right to be happy. It had been deceived many times and it looked upon the past with real horror. This country believed—blindly—that such a past could not return; the people were proud of their love of liberty and they carried their heads high in the conviction that liberty would be respected as a sacred right; they felt confident that no one would dare commit the crime of violating their democratic institutions. They desired a change for the better, aspired toward progress; and they saw all this at hand. All their hope was in the future.

My poor country! One morning the citizens awakened dismayed; under the cover of night, while the people slept, the ghosts of the past had conspired and now had seized the citizen body by the limbs . . . by its very throat. That grip, those claws were familiar: those jaws, those death dealing scythes, those boots. No; it was no nightmare; it was a sad and terrible reality: A man named Fulgencio Batista had just committed the appalling crime that no one had expected.

36

Then a humble citizen of this country, a citizen who longed to believe in the laws of the Republic and in the integrity of its judges, whom he had seen vent their fury against the underprivileged—opened a code of Social Defense to see what punishment society prescribed for the author of such a coup and he discovered the following:—

"Whosoever shall perpetrate any deed destined through violent means directly to change in whole or in part the Constitution of the State or the form of established government shall incur a sentence of six to ten years in jail."

"A sentence of three to ten years in jail will be decreed to the author of any act directed to promote an armed uprising against the Constitutional powers of the State. The sentence increases from five to twenty years if the insurrection is carried out."

"Whosoever shall perpetrate an act with the specific purpose of preventing, in whole or in part, even temporarily, the Senate, the Chamber of Representatives, the President or the Supreme Court from exercising their constitutional functions will incur a sentence from six to ten years in jail. Whosoever shall attempt to impede or tamper with the normal course of general elections, will incur a sentence from four to eight years in jail."

"Whosoever shall introduce, publish, distribute or attempt to carry out in Cuba any dispatch, order or decree tending to provoke the non-observance of the law will incur a sentence from two to six years in jail."

"Whosoever shall assume command of troops,

posts, fortresses, military camps, towns, warships or aircraft, without the authority to do so, or without express Government orders, will incur a sentence from five to ten years in jail."

A similar sentence will be passed upon anyone who usurps the exercise of a function held by the Constitution as properly belonging to the powers of State.

With Code in one hand and deposition in the other, that citizen went in our capital to the old building which housed the competent Court which was under obligation to bring cause against and punish those responsible for this deed. He presented a writ denouncing the crimes and asking that Fulgencio Batista and his seventeen accomplices be sentenced to from one to eight years in jail as decreed by the Code of Social Defense [for their crime], aggravated by second offense treachery and acting under cover of night.

Days and months passed by. What a disappointment! The accused remained unmolested; he strode up and down the country like a great lord and was called honorable sire and general: he removed and replaced judges at will. The very day that the court opened, the criminal occupied the seat of honor in the midst of our august and venerable patriarchs of justice.

37

Once more the days and the months rolled by, the people wearied of mockery and abuses. There is a limit to tolerance! The struggle began against this man who was disregarding the law, who had usurped power by the use of violence against the will of the people, who was guilty of aggression against the established order, and who tortured, murdered, imprisoned and prosecuted those who had taken up the fight to defend the law and to restore liberty to the people.

Honorable Magistrates, I am that humble citizen who one day came in vain to punish the power hungry men who had violated the law and had torn our institutions to shreds. Now that it is I who am accused, for attempting to overthrow this *illegal* regime and *to restore the legitimate constitution*, I am held for 76 days and am denied the right to speak to anyone, even to my son: guarded by two heavy machine guns, I am led through the city. I am transferred to this hospital to be tried secretly with the greatest severity; and the prosecutor with the Code in his hand, solemnly demands that I be sentenced to 26 years in prison.

You will answer that on the former occasion the courts failed to act because force prevented them from doing so. Well then—confess: this time force will oblige you to condemn me. The first time you were unable to punish the guilty: now you will be compelled to punish the innocent. The maiden of justice twice raped by force!

38

And such garrulity to justify the unjustifiable, to explain the inexplicable and to reconcile the irreconcilable!

The regime has reached the point of asserting that might-makes-right is the supreme law of the land. In other words that using tanks and soldiers to take over the Presidential palace, the national treasury, and the other government buildings and aiming guns at the heart of the people entitles them to govern the people! The same argument the Nazis were able to use when they occupied the nations of Europe and installed puppet governments in them.

I heartily agree that *revolution* can be the source of legal right: *but the nocturnal armed assault of the tenth of March could never be classified as a revolution*. In everyday language, as José Ingenieros said, it is common to give the name of revolution to small disorders promoted by a group of dissatisfied persons in order to grab, from those in power, both the political plums and the economic advantages. The usual result is no more than a change of hands in the divvying up of jobs and benefits. This is not the criterion of a philosopher of history, as it cannot be that of a cultured man.

Leaving aside the question of profound changes in the social system, not even on the surface of the public quagmire were we able to discern the slightest motion that could lessen the rampant putrefaction. The previous regime was guilty of petty politics, theft, pillage, and disrespect for human life; but the present regime increased political skullduggery five-fold, pillage ten-fold, and has increased a hundred-fold the lack of respect for human life. It was known that Barriguilla had plundered and

murdered, that he was a millionaire, that he owned in
Havana a good many apartment houses, countless stocks
in foreign companies, fabulous accounts in American
banks, that he distributed capital gains to the tune of
eighteen million dollars, that he was a frequent guest in
the most lavishly expensive hotels for tycoons. No one
would ever accept that Barriguilla was a revolutionist.
Barriguilla was that sergeant of Weyler who dispatched
twelve Cubans in El Guatao. *Bastista's* men murdered
seventy in Santiago de Cuba. *De te fabula narratur.*

39

Four political parties governed the country prior to
the tenth of March: the Auténtico, Liberal, Democratic
and Republican parties. Two days after the coup the Republican party changed sides. A year had not yet passed
by before the Liberal and Democratic parties were again
in power: Batista did not restore the Constitution, did
not restore civil liberties, did not restore Congress, did
not restore universal suffrage, did not restore in the end
any of the uprooted democratic institutions. But he *did*
restore Verdeja, Guas Inclán, Salvito García Ramos,
Anaya Murillo and the top heirarchy of the traditionally
government parties, the most corrupt rapacious, reac-
tionary and antediluvian elements of Cuban politics.
This was [like] the "revolution" of Barriguilla.

Lacking the most fundamental revolutionary orien-
tation Batista's regime represents in all respects a regres-
sion of twenty years for Cuba. Batista's return has ex-

acted a high price from all of us—but primarily from the lower classes which are suffering hunger and misery. Meanwhile the dictatorship has laid waste the nation with agitation, ineptitude and tottering economies and now engages in the most loathsome forms of ruthless politics, concocting formula after formula to perpetuate itself in power even if over a stack of corpses and a sea of blood.

Batista's regime has not set in motion a single nationwide program of betterment for the people. Batista delivered himself into the hands of the [selfish]. Little else could be expected from a man of his mentality—utterly devoid, as he is, both of ideals and of principles and utterly lacking, as he does, the faith, confidence, or backing of the masses. His regime brought merely a switch of hands and a re-distribution of loot among a new collection of friends, relatives, accomplices and parasitical dregs that constitute the political retinue of a Dictator. What great opprobium the people have been forced to endure so that a small clan of egotists altogether indifferent to the needs of their homeland may find in public life an easy and indulgent *modus vivendi*.

40

How right Eduardo Chibas was in his last radio speech when he said that Batista was encouraging the return of the colonels of castor oil[1] and of the *ley fuga*. Immediately after the tenth of March, Cubans began once more to witness such acts of veritable vandalism as they had considered banished forever from Cuba. There was an unprecedented attack on a cultural institution. The University of the Air was stormed by the thugs of the SIM, together with the young hoodlums of PAU.[2] There was also the case of Mario Kuchilan, dragged away from his home in the middle of the night and bestially tortured till he was nearly unconscious and the murder of student Rubén Batista and the criminal volleys fired at a peaceful student demonstration next to the same wall where the Spanish volunteers executed the students of 1871. And, many many cases such as that of Dr. García Bárcenas, when right in the courtrooms men have coughed up blood because of the barbaric tortures visited upon them by the repressive security forces. I will not enumerate the hundreds of cases where groups of citizens have been brutally clubbed—men, women, children and the aged.

All of this was being done even before the 26th of July. Since then, as everybody knows, Cardinal Arteaga[3] himself was not spared such treatment. According to the

[1]Refers to torture method Batista's first regime introduced into Cuba. Prisoners were given massive doses of castor oil, to subject them to intense intestinal pain and to overwhelming sensations of helplessness, as well as to filth.

[2]Partido Acción Unitaria. Political party of Batista.

[3]Manuel Cardinal Artega, prince of the Catholic Church.

official story, he was the victim of a "band of thieves."
For once the regime told the truth. What else are they?

41

Cuba has just witnessed with horror the case of the journalist who was kidnapped and subjected to torture by fire for twenty days. Each case brought forth evidence of unheard of effrontery, of immense hypocrisy: the cowardice of shirking responsibility and invariably blaming the enemies of the regime. Governmental tactics fit to be envied by the worst gangster mobs. Even the Nazi criminals were never so cowardly. Hitler assumed responsibility for the massacres of June 30th[1] 1934, stating that for 24 hours he had been the German Supreme Court: the henchmen of *this* dictatorship, which defies all comparison with others, due to its baseness, maliciousness and cowardice: kidnap, torture and murder and then loathsomely put the blame on the adversaries of the regime. The typical tactics of Sgt. Barriguilla!

Not once in all the cases I have mentioned, Honorable Magistrates have the agents accountable for them been brought forth to be tried by courts. How is this? Is this not the regime of public order peace and respect for human life?

[1]Date of Hitler's first political purge after assuming the Chancellorship wherein Roehm and other dissidents were assassinated.

42

I have recited all this in order now to ask you: Did Batista's present regime—his "revolution" of last year—ever have any of the rightful attributes of a real revolution? Is it or is it not constitutional to struggle against his regime? And must there not be a high degree of corruption in the courts of law when these courts imprison the citizens who try to rid their country of so much infamy?

Cuba is suffering a cruel and base despotism. You are well aware that resistance to despots is legitimate. This is a universally recognized principle and our Constitution of 1940[1] expressly makes it a sacred right, in the second paragraph of Article 40: "It is legitimate to use adequate resistance to protect previously granted individual rights."

And even if this prerogative had not been provided by the Supreme Law of the Land, it is a consideration without which one cannot conceive the existence of democratic societies. Professor Infiesta,[2] in his book on Constitutional Law, differentiates between the political and the judicial constitutions, and states: "Sometimes the Judicial Constitution includes constitutional principles which, even without being so classified, would be equally binding just on the basis of the people's consent, for example, the principle of majority rule in our democracies. The right of insurrection in the face of tyranny is one of such principles, and, whether or not it be included in the Judicial Constitution, it is always binding

[1] Document drafted by the *Asamblea Constituyente*, famous for its advanced social legislation.
[2] Professor of constitutional law at the University of Havana.

within a democratic society. The presentation of such a case to a high court is one of the most interesting problems of Civil Law.

Duguiit[3] has said in his Treaty on Constitutional Law: "If an insurrection fails, no court will dare to rule that this unsuccessful insurrection was technically *no* conspiracy or transgression against the security of the state inasmuch as, the government being tyrannical, the intention to overthrow it was legitimate."

But please take note. Duguiit does not state, "the court ought not to rule." He says, "no court will dare to rule." More explicitly he means that no court will *dare,* that no court will have enough courage to do so, under a tyranny. The issue admits no alternatives. If the court is courageous and does its duty, *yes,* it *will* dare.

43

Recently there has been a violent controversy concerning the validity of the constitution of 1940. The Court of Social and Constitutional Rights ruled against it in favor of the laws [that were unconstitutional under that constitution.] Nevertheless, Honorable Magistrates, I maintain that the 1940 constitution is still in power.

My statement may seem absurd and extemporaneous to you. But do not be surprised. It is I who am astonished that a court of law should have attempted to deal a

[3]French jurist.

vile death blow to the legitimate Constitution of the Republic. As I have done all along—strictly adhere to the facts, to truth, and to reason—I will prove what I have just affirmed.

The Court for Social and Constitutional Rights was instituted according to Article 172 of the 1940 Constitution, complemented by Organic Law Number 7 enacted on May 31, 1949. These laws, in virtue of which the Court was created, granted it, in questions of unconstitutionality, a specific and clearly defined area of legal competence: to rule in all matters of appeals claiming the unconstitutionality of all laws, legal decrees, revolutions or acts that negate, diminish, restrain or adulterate the constitutional rights and privileges or that jeopardize the operations of state agencies.

Article 194 established the following very clearly: "All judges and courts are under obligation to find solution to conflicts between the Constitution and the existing laws in accordance with the principle that the former shall always prevail above the latter."

According, therefore, to the laws that created it, the Court of Social and Constitutional Rights should always rule in favor of the Constitution. When this Court caused the statutes to prevail above the Constitution of the Republic, it completely overstepped its boundaries and its established field of competence, thereby rendering a decision which is legally null and void.

Furthermore, the decision in itself is absurd, and absurdities have no validity, neither by right nor by might—nor even from a metaphysical viewpoint. No matter how venerable a court may be, it cannot assert that circles are square—or what amounts to the same thing,—affirm that the grotesque offspring of Batista's, the April 4th statutes, should be considered the official Constitution.

The Constitution is understood to be the basic and supreme law of the land—to define the country's political structure, regulate the functioning of government agencies and determine the boundaries of their activities. It must be *sui generis*, stable, enduring—and to a certain extent inflexible. The statutes [of April 4th] fulfill none of these qualifications. To begin with, they harbor a monstruous, shameless and brazen contradiction in regard to the most vital subject—the integration relation of the Republican structure and the principle of national sovereignty.

Article I says: "Cuba is a sovereign and independent state constituted as a democratic Republic . . . Article II says: "Sovereignty resides in the will of the people, and all powers derive from this source."

But then comes Batista's Article 118 which says: "The President will be nominated by the Cabinet." So it is *not* the people who choose the president, but rather the Cabinet chooses him. And who chooses the Cabinet?

Batista's Article 120, section 13: "The President will be authorized to nominate and reappoint the members of the Cabinet and to replace them when the occasion arises." So, after all, who nominates whom? Is this not the old classic of the chicken and the egg that no one has ever been able to solve?

44

One day eighteen rogues got together. Their plan was to assault the Republic and loot its 350 million dollar annual budget. Treacherously and surreptitiously they succeeded in their purpose. "And what do we do next?" they wondered.

One of them said to the rest: "You name me Prime Minister and I will make you generals." As soon as this was done, he rounded up a claque of twenty men and told them: "I will make you my Cabinet and you will make me President."

In this fashion they nominated each other generals, ministers and president and then took over the treasury and government, lock, stock, and barrel.

Further, it was not simply a matter of the usurpation of sovereignty for one single time in order to name a Cabinet, a staff and a President. This man ascribed to himself, through these statutes, not only absolute control of the nation but also the power of life and death over every citizen and control over the very existence of the nation. Because of this, I maintain that the position of the Court of Social and Constitutional Rights is not only treacherous, vile, cowardly and repugnant, but also absurd.

Batista's statutes contain an article that has not received much attention but which furnishes the key to this situation and is the one from which we shall derive decisive conclusions. I refer specifically to the modifying clause included in Article 257, which reads: "This constitutional law is open to reform by the Cabinet by a two-thirds quorum vote." Here mockery reached its maximum.

Not only did they exercise sovereignty in order to impose upon the people a Constitution without the people's consent and to install a regime which concentrates all power in its own hands; but also, through Article 257, they assume the most essential attribute of sovereignty—the power to change the basic and supreme Law of the Land. And they have already changed it several times since the 10th of March. Yet, with the greatest gall, they assert in Article II that sovereignty resides in the will of the people and that the people are the source of all power.

Since these changes can be brought about by a vote of two-thirds of the Cabinet and the Cabinet is named by the president, then the right to make and break Cuba is in the hands of one man, a man who is, furthermore, the most unworthy of all the creatures ever born in this land.

Was this then accepted by the Court of Constitutional Rights? And is all that derives from it valid and legal? Very well, you shall see what was accepted:

"This constitutional law will be liable to change by a two-thirds quorum vote of the Cabinet." Such a power recognizes no limits. Under its aegis, any article, any chapter, any clause—even the whole law—can be modified. For example, Article I which I have just mentioned says that Cuba is a sovereign and independent state constituted as a democratic Republic, although today it is in fact a bloody satrapy. Article III reads: "The national boundaries include the island of Cuba, the Isle of Pines, and the neighboring islets and keys . . . " and so on.

Batista and his cabinet under the provisions of Article 257 can modify all these other articles. They can say that Cuba is no longer to be a Republic but a hereditary

107

monarchy and he, Batista, can anoint himself king. He can dismember the national territory and sell a province to a foreign country, as Napoleon did with Louisiana. He can suspend the right to life itself, and, like Herod, order the decapitation of newborn children. All of these measures would be legal and you, my friends, would have to incarcerate all those who opposed them, just as you now intend to do with me.

45

I have put forth extreme examples to show how sad and who humiliating is our present situation. To think that all those absolute powers are in the hands of men truly capable of selling our country with all its citizens! Since the Court of Constitutional Rights has accepted Batista's unconstitutional statutes, what more are they waiting for? They may as well hang up their judicial robes.

It is a fundamental principle of Civil Law that there can be no unconstitutionality where the Executive and the Legislative powers reside in the same body. When the Cabinet makes the laws, the decrees and the rules—and at the same time has the power to change the Constitution in ten minutes' time—then why the devil do we need a Court of Constitutional Rights?

The ruling in favor of Batista's statutes is irrational, inconceivable, illogical and contrary to the republican laws that you, Honorable Magistrates, swore to uphold. When the Court of Constitutional Rights supported

Batista's statutes against the Constitution, the Supreme Law of the Land was not abolished [as it seemed to be] but rather, the Court of Constitutional Rights renounced its autonomy and committed legal suicide. May it rest in peace.

46

The right to revolt, established in Article 40 of the Constitution, is still valid. Was it established to function while the Republic was enjoying normal conditions? No. This provision is, in relation to the Constitution, what a lifeboat is to a ship on high sea. The lifeboat is lowered only when, for example, the boat is torpedoed by enemies in ambush along its course. With our Constitution betrayed and the people deprived of all their prerogatives there was only one right left, one right which no power may abolish—the right to resist oppression and injustice.

If any doubt remains, there is an article of the Social Defense Code which the Honorable Prosecutor would have done well not to forget. It reads, I quote: "The appointed or elected government authorities that fail to resist sedition with all the available means will be liable to a sentence of from six to eight years."

The Judges of our nation were under obligation to resist Batista's treacherous military coup of the 10th of March. It is obvious that when no one else has observed the law and when nobody else has done his duty, then now, those who have observed the law and have done their duty should be sent to jail. [Sic!]

You will not be able to deny that the regime forced upon the nation is unworthy of Cuban tradition, unworthy of Cuba's history.

In his book, *The Spirit of Laws* which is the foundation of the modern division of governmental power, Montesquieu[1] makes a distinction between three types of government according to their basic natures: "The Republican form wherein the whole people or a portion thereof has sovereign power: the Monarchial form where only one man governs, but in accordance to fixed and well defined laws: and the despotic form where one man without regard for laws and rules acts as he pleases, regarding only his own will or whim."

Afterwards he adds: "A man whose five senses constantly tell him that he is everything and that the rest of humanity is nothing is bound to be lazy, ignorant and sensuous." As virtue is necessary to a democracy, and honor to a monarchy—fear is of the essence to a despotic regime, where virtue is not needed and honor would be dangerous."

[1]Charles de Secondat 1689–1755. French lawyer and political philosopher.

47

The right of rebellion against tyranny, Honorable
Magistrates, has been recognized from the most ancient
times to the present day by men of all creeds, ideas, and
doctrines.

In the theocratic monarchies of remote antiquity, in
China, it was in effect a constitutional principle that
when a King governed rudely and despotically he should
be deposed and replaced by a virtuous prince.

The philosophers of ancient India upheld the principle of active resistance to arbitrary authority. They
justified revolution and very often put their theories into
practice. One of their spiritual leaders used to say
that—"An opinion held by the majority is stronger than
the king himself. A rope weaved of many strands is
strong enough to drag a lion."

The city-states of Greece and republican Rome not
only admitted but defended the meting-out of violent
death to tyrants.

In the Middle Ages, John of Salisbury[1] in his *Book
of the Statesman* says that when a prince does not govern
according to law and degenerates into a tyrant, violent
overthrow is legitimate and justifiable. He recommends
for tyrants the dagger rather than poison.

Saint Thomas Aquinas, in the *Summa Theologica*,
rejects the doctrine of tyrannicide, and yet upholds the
thesis that tyrants should be overthrown by the people.

Martin Luther proclaimed that when a government
degenerates into a tyranny violating the laws, the subjects are released from their obligation to obey. His dis-
ciple, Philippe Melancthon, upholds the right of resis-

[1]English ecclesiastic. d. 1180.

tance when governments become despotic. Calvin, the most outstanding thinker of the Reformation, with regard to political ideas, postulates that people are entitled to take up arms to oppose any usurpation.

No less a man than Juan Mariana, a Spanish Jesuit during the reign of Philip II, asserts in his book, *De Rege et Regis Institutione*, that when a governor usurps power, or even if he were elected, when he governs in a tyrannical manner, it is licit for a private citizen to exercise tyrannicide, either directly or through subterfuge, with the least possible disturbance.

The French writer François Hotman[2] maintained that between the government and its subjects there is a bond or contract, and that the people may rise in rebellion against the tyranny of governments when the latter violate said agreement.

During that same historical era, a widely read booklet appeared under the title *Vindiciae Contra Tyrannos* and over the pseudonym, Stephanus Junius Brutus. It openly proclaimed that resistance to governments is legitimate when rulers oppress the people and that it is the duty of honorable judges to lead the struggle.

The Scottish reformers, John Knox and John Poynet, upheld the same point of view. And, in the most important book of that movement, George Buchanan stated that if a government achieves power without taking into account the consent of the people, or if a government rules their destiny in an unjust and arbitrary fashion, then that government becomes a tyranny and can be de-

[2] 1524—1590. Many of his writings brought changes in the study and teaching of law.

vested of power or in a final recourse, can have its leaders executed.

John Althus, a German jurist of the early Seventeenth Century states, in his *Treatise on Politics*, that sovereignty, as the supreme authority of the State, is born from the voluntary concourse of all its members; that governmental authority stems from the people and that its unjust, illegal or tyrannical function exempts them from the duty of obedience and justifies their resistance or rebellion.

Thus far, Honorable Magistrates, I have mentioned examples from antiquity, from the Middle Ages and from the beginnings of the modern age. I selected these examples from writers of all creeds.

Moreover, as you can see, the right to rebellion is at the very roots of Cuba's existence as a nation. By virtue of [a rebellion fifty years ago] you are today able to appear in the robes of Cuban magistrates. Would that those garments served the cause of justice!

48

It is well known that in England during the Eighteenth Century two kings, Charles I and James II, were dethroned for despotism. These acts coincided with the birth of liberal political philosophy and provided the ideological foundation for a new social class, which was then struggling to break the bonds of feudalism.

Against divine right autocracies this new philosophy upheld the principle of the social contract and of the consent of the governed, and constituted the foundation of the American Revolution of 1775 and of the French Revolution of 1789. These great events ushered in the liberation of the Spanish colonies in the New World— the final link in that chain being broken by Cuba.

The new philosophy nurtured our own political ideas and helped us evolve our Constitution from the Constitution of Guáimaro up to the Constitution of 1940. The latter was influenced by the socialist currents of our time; into it were built the principle of the social function of property and of man's inalienable right to that decorous living which large vested interests have [often] prevented him from realizing fully.

The right of insurrection against tyranny then underwent its final consecration and became a fundamental tenet of political liberty.

As far back as 1649 John Milton wrote that political power lies in the people, who can enthrone and dethrone kings and who have the *duty* of overthrowing tyrants.

John Locke, in his essay on government sustains that when the natural rights of man are violated, the people have the right and the duty of suppressing or changing the government. "The last recourse against wrongful and unauthorized force is opposition to it."

Jean Jacques Rousseau says with great eloquence in his *Social Contract:* "While a people sees itself forced to obey and obeys, it does well; as soon as it can shake off the yoke and shakes it off, it does better, recovering its liberty through use of the very right that had been taken away from it.

"The strongest man is never sufficiently strong to be always the master, but rather tries to convert force into right and tries to convert obedience into duty. Force is a physical power. I do not see what morality can be derived from its use. To cede to force is an act of necessity, not of will. All else is an act of prudence. In what sense can this be a duty?

"To renounce freedom is to renounce one's status as a man, to renounce one's human rights, including one's duties. There is no possible compensation for renouncing *everything*. Total renunciation is incompatible with the nature of man and to take away all free will is to take away all moral conduct. In short, it is vain and contradictory to stipulate on one hand an absolute authority and on the other hand an unlimited obedience.

Thomas Paine said that a just man deserves more respect than a crowned rogue. The people's right to rebel has been opposed only by reactionaries like that clergyman of Virginia, Jonathan Boucher,[1] who said that "The right to rebel is a censurable doctrine derived from Lucifer, the father of rebellions."

49

The Declaration of Independence of the Congress of Philadelphia, on the 4th of July, 1776, consecrated this right in a beautiful paragraph which reads:

" . . . We hold these truths to be self-evident, that all men are created equal, that they are endowed by

[1]1738—1804. English clergyman in the American colonies, who so opposed the American Revolutionary movement from his pulpit that he was forced to resign his parish and return to England.

their Creator with certain unalienable Rights, that among these are Life, Liberty, and the Pursuit of Happiness—That to secure these Rights, Governments are instituted among Men, deriving their just powers from the consent of the governed, that whenever any Form of Government becomes destructive of these ends, it is the Right of the People to altar or abolish it, and to institute new Government, laying its foundation on such principles and organizing its power in such form, as to them shall seem most likely to effect their Safety and Happiness."

The famous French Declaration of the Rights of Man willed this principle to the coming generations:

"When the government violates the rights of the people, insurrection is for them the most sacred of rights and the most imperative of duties." "When a person seizes sovereignty, he should be condemned to death by free men."

I believe I have sufficiently justified my point of view. I have called forth more reasons than the Honorable Prosecutor called forth to ask that I be condemned to 26 years in prison. All support men who struggle for freedom and happiness of the people. None support those who oppress the people, revile them and loot them heartlessly. Therefore, I have had to call forth many reasons and he could not adduce a single one.

How can you justify the presence of Batista in power, since he gained power against the will of the people and by violating the laws of the Republic through the use of treachery and force?

How can you qualify as legitimate a regime of blood, oppression, and ignominy? How can you call a regime revolutionary when it has combined the most backward men, the most backward ideas and the most backward bureaucracy? How can you consider legally valid the high treason of a court whose mission was to defend our constitution?

With what right do the courts send to prison citizens who tried to redeem their country by giving their own blood—their own lives?

All this is monstruous in the eyes of the nation and is monstruous according to the principles of true justice.

50

But there is one argument that aids us more than all the others. We are Cubans and to be Cuban implies a duty. Not to fulfill that duty is a crime, is treason.

We are proud of the history of our country. We learned history in school and we have grown up hearing of liberty, justice and human rights.

We were taught to venerate the glorious example of our heroes and our martyrs. Cespedes, Agramonte, Maceo, Gomez y Marti were the first names engraved in our minds. We were taught that the titan Maceo had said that liberty is not begged but is won with the blade of a machete.

We were taught that for the guidance of Cuba's free citizens the *Apóstol* wrote in his *Book of Gold:*[1] "The man who conforms by obeying unjust laws and permits

[1] A collection of stories in magazine form that Jose Martí prepared for children.

anybody to trample the country in which he was born, the man who so mistreats his country, is not an honorable man."

"In the world there must be a certain degree of decorum just as there must be a certain amount of light. When there are many men without decorum, there are always others who bear in themselves the dignity of many men. These are the men who rebel with great force against those who steal the people's freedom—that is to say, against those who steal human dignity itself."

We were taught that the 10th of October[2] and the 24th of February[3] are glorious anniversaries of national rejoicing because they mark days in which Cubans rebelled against the yoke of infamous tyrannies.

We were taught to cherish and defend the beloved flag of the single star. We sang every afternoon a hymn whose verses say that to live in chains is to live in opprobrium . . . that to die for the country is to live.

All this we learned and will never forget, even though today in our land there is murder and prison for the men who practice the ideas taught to them since the cradle. We were born in a free country which was our heritage from our forefathers. The island would sink into the sea before we would consent to be slaves of *anybody*.

[2]October 10, 1868, when cry of "Yara" began struggle for freedom from Spain.
[3]February 24, 1895 was the date that opened Cuba's final struggle for independence from Spain.

51

It seemed that the veneration for the Apóstol was going to die in his Centenary. It seemed that his memory would be extinguished forever. So great was the affront! But his dream lives. It has not died. His people are rebellious. His people are worthy. His people are faithful to his memory. There are Cubans who have fallen defending his doctrines. There are boys who in magnificent selflessness came to die beside his tomb, giving their blood and their lives so that [the dream of Marti] could continue to live in the heart of his country. Cuba, what would have become of you if you had forsaken your Apóstol?

I come to the close of my defense plea but I will not end it as lawyers usually do—asking that the accused be freed. I cannot ask freedom for myself while my comrades are suffering in the ignominious prison of *Isla de Pinos*. Send me there to join them and to share their fate. It is understandable that honest men should be dead or in prison in [this] Republic where the president is a criminal and a thief.

To the Honorable Magistrates, my sincere gratitude for having allowed me to express myself freely without petty interruptions, I hold no bitterness toward you. I recognize that in certain aspects you have been humane and I know that the Presiding Officer of this court, a man of unimpeachable private life, cannot disguise his repugnance at the current state of affairs that oblige him to dictate unjust decisions.

Still, there remains for this hearing a more serious problem, the issues arising from the murder of seventy men—that is to say, the greatest massacre we have ever known. The guilty continue at liberty with a weapon in hand—a weapon which continually threatens the citizens. If all the weight of the law does not fall upon [the guilty] because of cowardice, or because of domination of the courts—and if then, all the magistrates and judges do not resign, I pity you. And I regret the unprecedented shame that will fall over the judicial system.

I know that imprisonment will be as hard for me as it has ever been for anyone—filled with cowardly threats and wicked torture. But I do not fear prison, just as I do not fear the fury of the miserable tyrant who snuffed life out of seventy brothers of mine.

Sentence me. I don't mind. *History will absolve me.*